# CONTENTS

# INTEGRATED AREA PLANNING

## A COLLABORATIVE APPROACH TO DECISION-MAKING

Edited by

**Ciaran Lynch, Catherine Corcoran,
Cora Horgan, Paul Keating, Bridget Kirwan,
Martin McCormack, Elisha McGrane,
Michael Ryan**

OAK·TREE·PRESS

Published by
Oak Tree Press
19 Rutland Street, Cork, Ireland
www.oaktreepress.com


© 2008 Tipperary Institute.


A catalogue record of this book is
available from the British Library.


ISBN 978-1-904887-20-1

Printed in Ireland by ColourBooks
on recycled paper, using vegetable inks.

# FIGURES

# AUTHORS

**CATHERINE CORCORAN** has worked in community and rural development programmes in Ireland and overseas. Her interest in participatory processes became particularly strong while working in Africa with communities that had to develop their own governance systems in the virtual absence of the State. Catherine was a facilitator on a number of the IAPs outlined in this book and presently is working with organisations in Galway and Offaly that are interested in involving local communities more deeply in the planning process.

**CORA HORGAN** is employed currently as the CEO of Tipperary Regional Youth Service. Cora has extensive experience of social inclusion and organisational development. She was employed previously as a development officer with Ballyhoura Rural Development Company and with the Irish LEADER Support Unit.

**PAUL KEATING** works as a Programme Specialist with Tipperary Institute, where he teaches on the degree in Sustainable Rural Development. Paul has worked as a civil engineer with local authorities in Ireland and overseas on projects with Concern. He completed a Masters in Rural Development at UCD in 1997 and, since then, has worked with rural development organisations in Ireland under the CDP, LSDIP and LEADER programmes. In recent years, Paul has liaised closely with the Department of Community, Rural & Gaeltacht Affairs and the LEADER companies in providing support to that programme as manager of the Irish LEADER Support Unit. Since 2006, Paul has been involved in training, aimed at the strengthening of institutions to deliver rural development in the EU's new member states and other Eastern European countries.

**BRIDGET KIRWAN** works in the Centre for Developing Human Potential in Tipperary Institute. Bridget specialises in the areas of personal development and communication. Along with teaching at undergraduate level, she has been involved in a variety of outreach projects at community and business level. She also works in the area of group facilitation and organisational development. Earlier in her career, she worked as a trainer, training manager, and as a manager of a small business. Since working with the IAP process, she has become interested in exploring the challenge of participation from an individual perspective, especially the capacity of individuals to engage in the process and the challenge of including all groups in society.

**CIARAN LYNCH** is Head of the Rural Development Department and Director of Rural Development at Tipperary Institute, and was Director of the Irish LEADER Support Unit until the completion of the contract at the end of 2006. He is a graduate of UCD, the University of Wales and the Institute of Public Administration and has a background in social studies and physical planning, having worked for over 20 years as a town planner with a number of local authorities. He was the Chief Planner for 13 years with Clare County Council and was very involved in community planning and project development, as well as strategic planning. He presently works with a variety of public and community-based organisations on collaborative planning and development issues and has a broad experience in policy development and analysis, as well as a personal commitment to sustainable rural development and collaborative decision-making processes. He was the Project Manager for the preparation of the Mid-West Regional Authority's *Planning Guidelines* and has been involved in the National Spatial Strategy implementation.

**MARTIN McCORMACK** is an engineer by profession and, for many years, has worked as a trainer, adviser and facilitator with community groups involved in social and physical infrastructural development. Martin has worked also in Africa and is most interested in issues of social justice and in processes that equip people to deal better with the State and other agencies that make decisions about the physical environment. Martin was involved with most of the IAP processes outlined here, particularly in training communities in skills, such as mapping and planning, which enabled local people to participate more effectively in decision-making processes.

**ELISHA McGRANE** works as a Programme Specialist with Tipperary Institute, where she teaches environmental science. She is a graduate of NUI Maynooth and Trinity College Dublin. After completion of a Masters in 1992, she worked as an education officer in Wicklow Mountains National Park. Elisha has been involved in EU projects in the areas of waste management and education for sustainable development. She is very interested in education for sustainable development and how individuals and communities become empowered to address environmental issues that affect their lives. Elisha is particularly interested in the role that education can play in influencing people's behaviour and attitudes to the natural environment and the sustainable management of natural resources. She is currently co-ordinating a new honours science degree in Environmental & Natural Resource Management.

**MICHAEL RYAN** is a Programme Specialist in Human Development & Education Studies. He works as part of a team in Tipperary Institute, which has established the Centre for Developing Human Potential. The work of this team includes the development and facilitation of relevant modules for all full-time undergraduate students at the Institute and the development of customised human development outreach programmes for various groups and organisations. Michael has worked both in the formal educational sectors and with groups and organisations in the rural and community sectors. Currently, he is co-ordinating the education component of a Teacher Education degree programme and has a keen interest in capacity-building at individual and group levels.

# ACKNOWLEDGEMENTS

The development of this publication was truly a collaborative affair and is the result of a continuing and rich engagement between the staff of Tipperary Institute and the people we work with. We wish to acknowledge the enthusiasm and dedication of all the members of the community groups who participated in the Integrated Area Plans over the past seven years; their voluntary input provides the material upon which the plans are constructed. We also wish to acknowledge the very valuable input of time and resources dedicated to the project by the staff and elected members of local authorities, Partnership and LEADER companies and partner State and voluntary organisations. The approach taken to develop plans collaboratively requires time and demands a new way of working together. We hope you got as much out of the process as we did.

# INTRODUCTION

## Ciaran Lynch & Catherine Corcoran

Over the past seven years, Tipperary Institute (TI) has been commissioned by various local authorities and community groups to assist them in dealing with issues arising from the planning process. These groups were interested in drawing up local development plans and were interested in finding a less adversarial, and more positive, way of engaging in such processes. Since TI's central mission is the promotion of rural development, and given the importance of planning in the rural context, such involvement in planning has become an important focus for the Institute. This work has allowed staff members to develop a framework for local planning that has been called *Integrated Area Planning* (IAP).

This book explores the experiences of TI staff as they interacted with communities, local authorities and other key agencies in developing a collaborative approach to rural development. The proposition behind this book is that planning for rural areas is multi-faceted and, potentially, incorporates all aspects of rural community life. Traditional planning practice has focused almost exclusively on spatial development. Increasingly, however, it is recognised that a successful plan for an area's development cannot deal with spatial aspects in isolation from the social, environmental and economic issues that are crucial elements of rural community life. Also of importance is how decisions are made and who makes them.

The nature of planning and development in the rural areas of Ireland has become increasingly fraught in recent years. The rapid development of the Irish economy and subsequent demographic changes over the past two decades has led to increased demand for housing and infrastructure in most parts of the country. Issues relating to planning are causing major problems for many local authorities and are impacting at professional, political and managerial levels. There is a clear breakdown in trust, at many levels and in many areas, within the planning system. The objectives considered appropriate by technical planners, by policy managers, by politicians and by communities and individuals are often at odds and incompatible. This has led to a great deal of difficulty for all those involved.

## PLANNING ISSUES IN SMALL PLACES

Writers and practitioners concerned with collaborative planning maintain that place-specific matters are central to the planning process. Harris (2002) says that, paradoxically, most planning theory, because it is theory, is devoid of any historical, cultural or place-related references. In planning theory, because it is supposed to be applied anywhere, and because it is so closely aligned to public administration, issues of space and place often appear as additional attributes rather than as central concerns. The development of collaborative planning approaches, he argues, reasserts place-focused concerns in public policy generally. The inclusion of specific spatial awareness and local understanding into approaches to planning theory is one of the defining characteristics of collaborative planning (Harris, 2002, p.34).

Small urban centres, towns and villages, form the *locus* of the IAP and are a key feature of the Irish landscape. Traditionally, they have provided a base from which services, such as health, education and recreation, can be delivered. They have acted as an economic anchor for the rural hinterland. They have provided a physical focal point for community activity and for local identity. Their shops, post offices and halls have acted as places of service delivery and points of contact. Increasingly, these settlements are at risk, either of decline and service closure or of developing into anonymous suburbs or dormitories without a life of their own.

In rural development terms, the situation presents a significant challenge. Evidence from the last three censuses, and noted by Jackson & Haase (1996. p.75), shows the extent to which the fate of rural Ireland is determined by urban factors. What is called 'the interpenetration of the countryside by the urban shadow' is now evident, particularly around the major urban areas. A pattern of relative affluence and disadvantage is found and, as mapped by Jackson & Haase, these form concentric circles around Irish cities and towns. The core areas of towns and cities are becoming less populated and less important in economic terms, as new retail and industrial centres form in the suburban concentric ring. These suburban rings also form the nexus of population growth, as commuters are able to buy property at a lower cost than in the urban areas. Anecdotal evidence suggests that the middle classes are 'fleeing the urban' and moving to the suburban fringe or to one-off houses in the countryside, but as near as possible to the town, creating the new Irish landscape of unplanned suburbia. Towns and villages that fall within commuting distance of large urban centres are under pressure to become dormitory towns as they become part of the 'urban fringe'. And:

'… as the development of the urban fringe has continued, it has tended to worsen the situation of the propertyless and landless rural and urban population, as they have been forced to compete in a market inflated by affluent urban interests and a social structure and culture that is increasingly defined by affluent urban values'. (Jackson & Haase, 1996, p.76)

## TWO TYPES OF 'RURAL'?

This book examines the IAP process as it unfolded in four areas – Eyrecourt and Kinvara, Co. Galway; Ferbane, Co. Offaly; and Hacketstown, Co. Carlow – and draws on experiences in Crusheen, Co. Clare and Kilmacthomas, Co. Waterford. These areas, all with populations of 1,500 or less, may be characterised broadly as being at risk of either:

◊ Decline and service closure (Eyrecourt, Ferbane and Hacketstown), or

◊ Becoming overshadowed and overwhelmed by their proximity to large urban areas (Kinvara, Crusheen and Kilmacthomas).

The areas at risk of decline (Eyrecourt, Ferbane and Hacketstown) displayed some or all of the following characteristics:

◊ Population decline or failure to grow to average national census levels.

◊ The loss of skilled young people to larger urban centres.

◊ The lack of real employment opportunities and of a significant skill-base within such communities, contributing to a decline in commercial and retail investment.

◊ The lack of sufficient demand for key services and social amenities, due to population decline.

◊ A skewing in population, resulting in higher numbers of age-dependent and unemployed people.

◊ A lack of investment in private housing development and thus lack of a sufficient consumer base for the development of local services and outlets.

The loss in population, and the absence of policy in terms of service provision in small rural towns and villages, triggers what Jackson & Haase call 'a principle of circular and cumulative causation' (1996, p.77). A cumulative cycle of disadvantage is set up, whereby outward migration, itself stimulated by employment opportunities elsewhere, leads to an unbalanced age structure and sex ratio that tends to a low marriage rate and a reduction in natural increase, as well as adding to the economic disadvantages already present on the supply side. These factors, in turn, reduce demand for key services, such as schools, clinics, childcare and transport, thereby stimulating further decline.

The three other areas that were the focus of IAP (Crusheen, Kinvara and Kilmacthomas) experienced a different set of issues:

◊ Increasing demand for housing in the area from people working in a nearby large urban area.

◊ Increasing demand on the capacity of the local infrastructure, such as water and sewerage schemes.

◊ Increasing demand for health, education and childcare services, to which the State had not adequately responded.

◊ Increasing traffic movement, leading to congestion and concerns about road safety.

◊   The incorporation of new residents, both Irish and non-national,
    into local society, without the necessary support systems.

Thus, in the opinion of Jackson & Haase, a particular type of population
movement has been occurring in Ireland over the past two decades: the
thinning-out of population in peripheral rural areas, and also in inner-
city areas, and settlement in outer urban belts within commuting
distances of the cities and towns:

> 'It is interesting to note that this population movement is not a
> phenomenon characteristic of any particular region or province,
> but encompasses the whole of Ireland and appears to reflect
> structural changes in the organisation of society as a whole. These,
> in turn, may result from the location of jobs, changes in travel-to
> work patterns, the increased availability of private transport, as
> well as the ready availability of new housing and planning
> permissions at the outskirts of existing population centres.'
> (Jackson & Haase, 1996, p.67)

These demographic changes are having a profound influence on rural
Ireland. It is difficult now to imagine just one 'type' of rural area. The
1999 *White Paper on Rural Development* (Department of Agriculture &
Food, 1999) defines 'rural' as all areas outside of the five major urban
centres. Under this definition, large towns such as Dundalk and Naas
are considered rural, in the same way as villages and small towns such
as Eyrecourt or Hacketstown. In the opinion of the authors of
*Community Work in a Rural Setting* (ADM, 2003, p.14), such definition
fails to recognise that the experience of rural life will differ significantly
from location to location, due to a number of factors including
population density, age structure, nature of the local economy, access to
services and distance from major urban centres.

On the other hand, the Central Statistics Office (CSO) describes rural
as being the 'open countryside', as well as towns of less than 1,500
persons. Under this definition, 42% of the population were living in
rural areas in 1996, 40.4% in 2002 and 39.3% in 2006 (CSO, 2007, p.14).
According to the most recent census report, the population living in
urban areas (in towns with a population of 1,500 or more) has increased
at every census since the foundation of the State. In the 10 years from

1996-2006, the urban population increased by 460,000 persons (CSO, 2007, p.13). Furthermore, the CSO notes that:

> '… the population living in rural areas has experienced a recovery in recent years following decades of decline, with the increase in the period 1996-2006 amounting to 150,000 … Notwithstanding the recent increase in the population of rural areas, the urban share of the population continued to grow. Interestingly, the trend towards increasing urbanisation is most evident in the towns rather than in the cities. The combined population of towns with a population of 10,000 or more is now over 600,000. Smaller towns with a population of 1,500 to 9,999 increased in population by 13.9%. This figure was well in excess of the national average for population growth in Ireland between the years 2002-06 of 8.2%.' (CSO, 2007, p.14)

It is to be noted that the CSO does not compile aggregate data concerning towns with a population of less than 1,500, which were the subject of the IAPs. It is clear that patterns of settlement, and the consequent social, environmental and economic impacts, are poorly understood and, therefore, would prove a rich seam for researchers into such processes.

## INTEGRATED AREA PLANNING IN ACTION

The theoretical and philosophical underpinning of the IAP framework lies within the realm of collaborative planning theory and practice. Collaborative planning focuses upon a concern with the democratic management and control of urban and regional environments and with the design of less oppressive planning mechanisms. Planning decisions are taken in the context of planning and development legislation in the Republic of Ireland, so it is important that the nature of these processes, and the extent to which they facilitate or hinder collaborative processes, should be examined. **Chapters 1** and **7** in this book by Ciaran Lynch explore these territories and provide a context for this publication.

Kinvara in Co. Galway was one location for an Integrated Area Plan. Many of the recent problems being experienced by residents of this rather lovely coastal town were as a result of rapid development pressure in the area, due to its many desirable features and its proximity to Galway city. Whilst Kinvara may have been subject to exceptional pressure, the environmental, economic and social issues facing the area were quite typical of many Irish towns and villages. The case study by Catherine Corcoran in **Chapter 2**, of the process of planning in Kinvara, explains how one community and its partners used the IAP process in attempting to tackle these issues. This chapter also explains how an IAP works in practice and the particular framework employed to encourage a collaborative approach at a local level.

In **Chapter 3**, *The Environment & the IAP Process*, Elisha McGrane explores the role of the IAP process in promoting environmental sustainability in rural areas. This chapter outlines why the involvement of communities in the decision-making process on issues relating to environmental sustainability is key. This is due both to the high priority given to environmental matters by many communities and the intimate knowledge local people have of their own natural and built environments. The recognition and formalisation of such local knowledge goes to the heart of the IAP process, which maintains that decision-makers must find ways of working effectively with local people, if proper decisions are to be made. Such mutual collaboration not only ensures better outcomes, but also allows communities to develop better working relationships with traditional power-holders, and allows both parties to address environmental concerns in a pro-active, non-confrontational way.

Michael Ryan, in **Chapter 4**, explores the issue of capacity-building, or the development of skills by individual participants, during an IAP process. Using a case study approach with one community group, the chapter explores whether, in this case, the IAP process developed the capacity of community members (who were the local drivers of the project) to become local development agents. IAP places an implicit value around the drawing-out or development of longer-term skills and capacities for steering group members. It is anticipated that these trained people will go on to reinvest this capacity in the community for future years. Through a programme of research that operated in parallel with the IAP, the researcher facilitated local participants to measure their own personal development against a set of criteria, such as analytical ability, research skills, networking capacity and communication skills. The process itself generated 12 capacity-building indicators and significant improvement was verified across each of these, throughout the process.

The research, therefore, suggests that the IAP process in this particular case did draw out unrecognised or dormant potential, by enhancing opportunities and access to resources. IAP, therefore, has the potential to develop the individual and collective capabilities of a steering group to act purposefully for positive change in their own community.

Bridget Kirwan, in **Chapter 5**, looks at IAP from the perspective of the individual community person elected onto a local group to co-ordinate the process. She explores some of the models and interpretations of participation as a concept. Her paper argues that participation is seen as having one or more of the following purposes:

◊  To develop equality between people.

◊  As a tool in developing personal autonomy or self-determination.

◊  As driving forward the concept of community.

◊  As a basis for self-development.

Using evidence from a number of theoretical psychological models, she proposes a typology for training of individuals through the IAP process that develops their skills as participants. She also explores the personality-based factors that may make participation easier for certain people than others. She also looks at exchange theory, theories of social comparison and of life-cycle, which suggest that participation in IAP processes is easier for those who already feel comfortable in positions of influence than for others who are not accustomed to such involvement. This may help to answer the ongoing issue as to why certain individuals, or people with a certain profile, such as the unemployed, under-25s, women from local authority estates or minority groups, find it more difficult to participate in local planning processes than others.

Martin McCormack, in **Chapter 6**, argues that an IAP process involves a complex match of technical information on issues such as land-use management, economic planning and infrastructure development, with 'people-based' processes such as community development and social service provision. IAP, therefore, requires a significant amount of data to be made available in a clear and accessible way to all stakeholders to allow more informed decision-making. Geographic Information Systems (GIS) help to provide information in a defined spatial context. By providing a visual representation of data, GIS helps people to look at information differently and has the potential to engage stakeholders in a more immediate way than, say, reading a long report. It allows stakeholders to reflect on the spatial nature and context of proposals and the development of options related to development planning and the adoption of best practicable options. The presentation of population growth trends on GIS, for example, can help to ensure better land-use planning and convince stakeholders about optimum density usage, the need to balance housing with increased recreational and amenity space and the development of adequate waste management infrastructure and practices. The author argues that the participation of community members in mapping exercises (such as identification of local sites/ features of importance, mapping of existing and proposed road and footpath options or siting of recreational facilities) ultimately can lead to a plan that has been 'proofed' to a higher degree than would otherwise be possible. Like Elisha McGrane, he argues that local ownership of the physical environment can be developed best through an increased understanding of, and participation in, processes aimed at helping to ensure environmental sustainability.

Paul Keating, in **Chapter 8**, explores the theme of participation in a different way, from the perspective of the crisis in representative democracy in Western countries and the need to build new relationships between local government and local people. Can the notion and practice of participatory development facilitate fundamental social change? Or is it viewed and used by the powerful as merely another means of contracting 'participants' into pre-conceived and centrally-controlled projects, thereby reinforcing the social structures that perpetuate inequity? Here in Ireland, the process of popular participation in governance has started to be institutionalised through various forms of social partnership at both national and local levels. Bodies such as LEADER companies, local area partnerships, county development boards and issue-based committees bring representatives of community interests together with those of the State and the market around a set of common objectives. However, tensions exist in these new relationships, particularly around the scale and pace of change in the decision-making process. The interface between community and the State is often most apparent in the planning process. With an increased requirement on statutory agencies to support public participation in planning, and with heightened capacity and expectation on the part of community-based organisations, attention is now turning to structural issues such as the capacity of State institutions to absorb such processes into their decision-making, or how to institutionalise participation into local government, since, in Chambers' words, 'empowerment can be weak, unless it is embodied in institutions' (Chambers, 1997). The challenge to the State is to begin the arduous process of re-orientating institutional policies, procedures and norms to allow true participatory democracy to flourish.

Cora Horgan, in **Chapter 9**, looks at the issue of social inclusion and social integration in the IAP process. An underlying challenge in rural planning is how to address inequalities between social groups, while also addressing the disadvantages faced by the community as a whole. This reflects an ongoing debate in addressing social exclusion that acknowledges the spatial, as well as the social/structural, causes of exclusion. Approaches to rural disadvantage have traditionally placed a strong emphasis on spatial disadvantage and an integrated approach is employed to raise the development of the community as a whole. Using an objective analysis of distribution of disadvantage certainly highlights particular rural areas in need of special attention. However, social exclusion of particular groups of people is not confined to the most visibly poor areas but is present in all areas and, in particular, in Ireland, is most likely to occur in small towns and villages, where such issues are often glossed over and rendered invisible. This invisibility is a major concern and tackling factors such as class, gender, income, age, family status, disability and ethnicity, without causing further stigmatisation, is a necessary prerequisite to tackling rural disadvantage. In addressing rural social exclusion then, it is necessary to address *both* spatial and social inequalities. The challenges facing the IAP process are to highlight social inclusion as a complementary feature of social integration, to identify the marginalised within a community, to support them to identify specific needs and to develop and implement responses to those needs in the context of developing a socially integrated development strategy. Failing to tackle issues of social exclusion may mean that the IAP process further excludes the powerless, if the mechanisms to include them are not in place. If IAP is really planning for the whole community, then it must emphasise those traditionally excluded to represent everyone equally.

# 1

# THE CONCEPT OF PARTICIPATION IN LAND–USE PLANNING

## *Ciaran Lynch*

## PARTICIPATION IN PLANNING IN IRELAND

The models of planning policy-making that have traditionally been used in Ireland, on the basis of anecdotal evidence at least, have led to high levels of dissatisfaction amongst communities, elected members, representative organisations and public officials alike.

Of course, this is not surprising, since the local government system, the planning system itself and the history of the country have tended to generate an adversarial, as opposed to a collaborative, approach to decision-making, which will be discussed further in the following chapter. This may not have been so critical in the past, when there was a greater consensus on outcomes, and when there was a general agreement on the overall thrust of policy. However, this consensus has been breaking down in Ireland over the last 20 years and the disagreements are becoming more and more strident.

With the introduction of the Planning & Development Act 2000, there is a requirement on planning authorities to produce their statutory plans through a process that involves greater public input at earlier stages. At whatever level, local authorities are now instructed to develop a somewhat more participatory approach to planning than was heretofore the case. The Planning & Development Act 2000 also provides a statutory basis for the making of local area plans, using a process similar to that for the more extensive strategic local development plans.

Partnership structures established to deal with issues emerging from uneven economic development, such as rural decline and unemployment also have been challenged, in the past few years, to deal with the increasing, and in some cases overwhelming, demand for housing in rural areas. Issues relating to planning are causing major problems for many local authorities in the country and are impacting on local authorities at professional, political and managerial levels (Lynch, 2003). There is a clear breakdown in trust, at many levels and in many areas. The objectives considered appropriate by technical planners, by policy managers, by politicians and by communities and individuals are often at odds and incompatible. This has led to a great deal of difficulty for all those engaged in this aspect of the planning process.

While planners and central government might insist on concentration of housing within towns and villages, rural and farming organisations argue that social sustainability demands that housing be located in the countryside; that the current practice of concentrating dwellings in the largest towns is restrictive; and that rural housing can contribute positively to the future well-being of villages (Lynch, 2003). It has been argued that one of the underlying causes of the disagreement in this area is the lack of a shared vision of what, and how, the rural areas of the country *should be*. While the planning process, as set out in the law, has many excellent characteristics, it lacks an effective process for the creation of the shared visions that must underlie any attempt to create a set of goals and policies that will have wide-spread consent.

This difficulty is symptomatic of a more endemic problem, inherent in the ways in which many of the policy decisions regarding local development are made. Often communities and other groups are asked to participate in discussions regarding the mechanisms for implementing visions that are decided elsewhere rather than being asked to participate in the setting of those visions. The involvement of local people as part of partnership structures is only likely to be meaningful, if those local structures have real power to make decisions (Frazer, 1996, p.51). If the visions and the goals can be agreed locally by the various interest groups, and if this process is accepted by the policy-makers, reaching consensus on the mechanisms is often far less difficult.

There are many ways that the requirement to involve local communities in the planning process can be fulfilled. At its most basic, local authorities can involve the community in a process of consultation around plans that are drawn up at a central level. Local people may be invited to participate in a planning process, by being consulted about what will happen in their area, and problems and solutions may be modified in the light of people's responses. This would involve a very low level of participation and might be labelled as tokenistic. At another, more significant level, local people can be invited to participate in a joint analysis of needs in tandem with the local authority, leading to the development of action plans and the formation of new local institutions or the strengthening of existing ones. The degree to which local actors could exercise power to make the target agencies responsive to their views, aspirations and needs is an important feature here. In effect, this model is based on the concept of developing a participatory and collaborative approach to planning.

## CONCEPTUALISING PARTICIPATION

The concept of a participatory approach that involves citizens in the planning process is not new. Arnstein's seminal work in the US in the late 1960s, while she was involved in developing processes for citizen participation in planning and urban renewal projects, has been highly influential, both in shaping participatory theory and collaborative planning approaches (Arnstein, 1969). Arnstein developed an eight-rung 'ladder of citizen participation', with each rung corresponding to the extent of citizens' power in determining the end product. At the bottom of the ladder are Rung 1: Manipulation and Rung 2: Therapy. Using these two rungs, she describes levels of non-participation that have been contrived by some to substitute for real participation, while really designed to 'educate' or 'cure' the participants. She uses rungs 3, 4 and 5 to illustrate progress to levels of tokenism that allow the 'have-nots' to hear and to have a voice, although, under these conditions, they lack the power to ensure that their views will actually be heeded by the powerful. Further up the ladder, Arnstein describes levels of citizen power with increasing degrees of citizen involvement in decision-making. At Rung 6, citizens can enter into a partnership that enables them to negotiate and engage in trade-offs with traditional power-holders. At the top-most rungs, Rung 7: Delegated power and Rung 8: Citizen control, 'have-not' citizens obtain the majority of decision-making seats or full managerial power. Thus Arnstein maintains that participation has significant gradations. The distinguishing factor in the typology is the degree of power that the 'have-nots' gain, in order to compel key institutions to become responsive to their views, aspirations and needs.

Another useful approach that provides a basis for analysing processes of decision-making in planning, is that developed by Innes & Booher (2000).

## Figure 1.1: Models of Decision-making

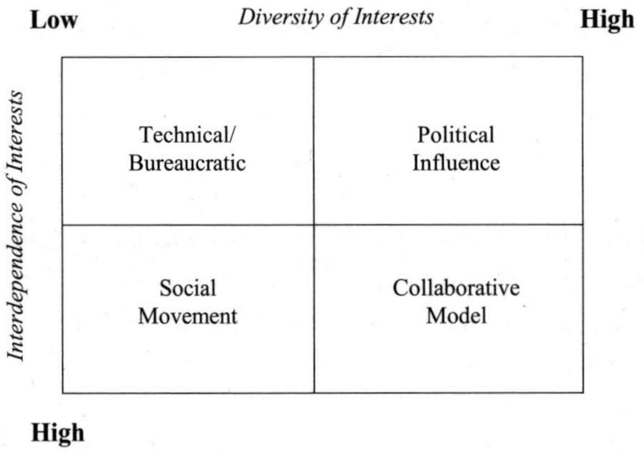

**Low**              *Diversity of Interests*              **High**

|  | Technical/ Bureaucratic | Political Influence |
|---|---|---|
|  | Social Movement | Collaborative Model |

*Interdependence of Interests*

**High**

After Innes & Booher (2000).

Innes & Booher propose the following:

'The *technical/bureaucratic* model works best where there is neither diversity nor interdependence among interests. Technicians and bureaucracies need to respond to a single set of goals and decision-maker and at least the typical practice is one where analyses are not focused on interdependencies (though this could change as more sophisticated technology and complexity modelling could permit this). The *political influence* model works well with diverse interests, but since each interest is focused on getting a piece of the pie and the political leader is busy amassing power, little or no horizontal dialogue takes place among interests. The *social movement* model is one which recognizes the importance of interdependence among a coalition of interests and individuals, but which does not deal with the full diversity of interests. *Collaboration* is the model that deals best with both diversity and interdependence but it is typically the least-used and least-institutionalized of the four models.' (Innes & Booher, 2000, p.20)

Within the technical/bureaucratic model, the focus of planning is on the achievement of the most efficient mechanisms for reaching easily-defined and identified ends. As Innes & Booher state:

'The technical bureaucratic model works well in conditions of comparative certainty, where there is only one interest — in effect, where there is agreement about the objectives and a single decision-making entity. Bureaucracy is set up to implement known policy and follow a hierarchical chain of authority. The technical analyst has come to be associated with rationality and bureaucracy. The education that planners and policy analysts in this tradition get typically begs the question of diverse goals and starts instead with a question that is simply about the best way to meet a predetermined goal.' (Innes & Booher, 2000, p.22)

Within the political influence model, there is an acknowledgement of some diversity of interests, but the recognition of interdependence is low. In this model, there tends to be a political bargaining approach that seeks to get an adequate number of interests to agree to a particular course of action in order for it to happen:

'The political influence model works well with diverse interests, but since each interest is focused on getting a piece of the pie, and the political leader is busy amassing power, little or no horizontal dialogue takes place among interests.' (Innes & Booher, 2000, p.20)

The technical/bureaucratic and political influence models of planning and decision-making, as proposed by Innes & Booher, reflect the lower levels of participation on the Arnstein ladder. Indeed, the 'convincing' behaviour of the Innes & Booher technical/bureaucratic model finds a great resonance in the 'educate' and 'cure' language of Arnstein's tokenism rungs.

As noted by Innes & Booher, however, a different model of planning and policy-making is needed in situations where there is a clear interdependence between stakeholders' interests and there exists a high diversity of such interests. Innes & Booher call this model 'collaborative planning':

> 'The collaborative model is about stakeholders co-evolving to a common understanding, direction and set of heuristics ... It is only the collaborative model that deals both with diversity and interdependence because it tries to be inclusive and to explore interdependence in the search for solutions. It does not ignore or override interests, but seeks solutions that satisfy multiple interests. It turns out, in our observation, that it is only the collaborative model that allows for genuinely regional, or other collectively beneficial, solutions to complex and controversial problems. For complex and controversial issues in rapidly changing and uncertain contexts – issues that there is public pressure to address – collaboration among stakeholders is likely to be the best approach – indeed, the only approach that can produce a satisfactory result.' (Innes & Booher, 2000, p.21)

Reflecting the Innes & Booher model, Healey also believes that a collaborative approach can be successful only when there is a variety of stakeholder interests, as, when all interests are the same, no dialogue is required.

Healey (1997) argues that collaborative planning has the following characteristics:

◊ Grounded in relation-building processes and is focused on relational webs or networks.

◊ Recognises that people operate across a multiplicity of networks and that the dynamic of social change arises through the mobilisation of such networks.

◊ Recognises that governance is far wider than government by formal institutions and is dependent upon a wide range of informal processes.

◊ Recognises that spatial planning can help to build up 'institutional capacity' (the quality of the relational networks within a locality).

◊ Recognises the importance of creating links at the level of neighbourhood, town and city, thus working to build up links across networks, improving relational capacity in these places.

◊ Builds upon a process of inclusionary argumentation that 'generates conviction'. This focuses upon how participants come together and establish a basis of trust and understanding.

◊ Involves communicative ethics that lead to a dialogue where there is a process of mutual learning, allowing for consensus-building, which in itself is specific to the time and place. This allows for conditions of cultural difference to be accommodated, and recognises that there is a diversity of ways of knowing.

◊ Recognises that building a strategic process by identifying key-stakeholders and relying on pre-existent groups leaves out those who have no voice in public arenas, and that an inclusionary ethic means that techniques need to be employed to overcome this problem. This can be a 'snowballing' technique, which encompasses those who come into contact with the process, or a stakeholder-mapping process.

◊ Should include a right to challenge decisions (in the UK, for example, there is not), and a right to call to account, which would help ensure that full collaboration took place.

◊ Needs a variety of resources to function properly and these should be made available. In addition, the system of governmental competencies needs to be reviewed.

Another approach to collaborative planning is that which emerges from the work of John Forester, who focuses on the communicative role of the planning analyst. His view is that planners within organisations do not work instrumentally towards the achievement of clearly-distinguishable ends. Instead, the role of the planning analyst is to:

'… work instead toward the correction of the needless distortions, some systematic and some not, which disable, mystify, distract and mislead others: to work towards a political democratisation of daily communications.' (Forester, 1989, p.21).

Further on in the same work, the author states that:

> '... problems will be solved not only by technical experts, but also by pooling expertise and non-professional contributions too; not just by formal procedure but also by informal consultation and involvement; not predominantly by strict reliance on databases, but also by careful use of trusted resources, contacts and friends; not mainly through formally rational management procedures, but through internal and external politics and the development of a working consensus; not by solving an engineering equation but by complementing technical performance with political sophistication, support building, liaison work – all this organising – and finally intuition and luck.' (Forester, 1989, p.152)

In all of this, Forester recognises the communication and negotiation elements of planning, as well as its technical elements. He recognises the political nature of planning and the extent to which the planner is engaged in value-laden political action.

These more participatory approaches to planning and policy-making now are being reflected in the more general environmental field. For example, a recent workshop reported that:

> 'The environmental assessment community is now taking on board participatory methods. For example, Integrated Assessment can bring together scientific and consultative approaches, accommodate the uncertainties and complexities of environmental issues, and include non-expert participants. If a process is to be fully participatory, stakeholders should not only receive information; they should supply their own facts and uncertainties. At the same time, the information with which they are provided must be useable and meaningful. They may need access to experts' information, and experts may need to learn from stakeholders. The process should be reflexive and ongoing, and decision-makers should be involved at all stages.' (Webster & Ougham, 1998)

Even when collaborative processes are used, however, land-use planning is likely to be a contested and conflicted activity, since, when decisions about the allocation of scarce natural resources are being made, there will always be those who seem to gain and those who seem to lose.

## CRITICS OF COLLABORATIVE PLANNING

While collaborative planning has been promoted as an appropriate approach to decision-making in complex environments, the process also has had many criticisms levelled at it. It is not the purpose of this chapter to provide an exhaustive list of these critiques. However, a number of the criticisms levelled at the process are well expressed by Fainstein (2000), who reflects on the following weaknesses in the approach:

◊ It is based on a functionalist, rather than a conflict, theory of society.

◊ It leads to the fudging of real issues, in order to achieve a nominal consensus that does not reflect reality.

◊ Action/implementation is often a problem, because the parties in the process are not honest about their intentions and purposes.

◊ It ignores the role of the powerful and their capacity to impede the implementation of agreed actions.

◊ If the planner/expert acts as a facilitator only, new and creative thinking can be stifled and only those solutions that are incrementalist in nature will emerge.

◊ The process is usually too drawn out and resource-hungry, and can lead to cynicism and it being viewed as a 'talking shop'.

◊ Stakeholder input can be excluding for the weak, as the NIMBY ('not-in-my-back-yard') effect will take hold and anything that changes the *status quo* in too extreme a manner will be excluded.

◊ There is evidence that experts acting on their own often come to better solutions than stakeholders operating in a collaborative process.

Pennington (2002) is another critic of the approach, whose principal objections are:

◊ **Logical:** The claim that 'complexly-related entities must be managed on a similarly holistic basis is a *non sequitur*', a premature and normatively-driven conclusion. 'On the contrary, … it is precisely because these systems are complexly-related wholes that conscious social control is … problematic'.

◊ **Epistemological:** Much of what drives human actions is tacit knowledge, 'time- and place-specific information that cannot be articulated in verbal form'. The idea to attempt co-ordination through verbal expression must necessarily skip crucial forms of knowledge because it is only revealed through action.

◊ **Cognitive:** Human interactions, especially at an urban/regional scale, are too complex to be understood, let alone steered. The human mind has 'cognitive limits' and their denial 'over-estimates the extent to which social co-ordination can be brought about by deliberative means'.

◊ **Logistical:** It is technically impossible to involve every single person. As a consequence, 'one might ... ask why ... the multitude of people, who for logistical reasons cannot be involved, should feel any more "empowered" than they might under the rule of technocratic procedures?'.

◊ **Substantive:** Deliberative approaches strangle innovation. If new ideas can be tried out, only if a general consensus approves of them, many good ideas will never come to fruition. In this sense, dissensus can be more productive than consensus (Pennington, 2002).

While there are undoubtedly issues associated with the concept of collaborative planning at a practical level, however, it is clear that the current approach to planning gives rise to too many difficulties. It might also be argued that some of the critiques of the collaborative planning model are based on consideration of their idealised formulations. It is arguable, and is proposed in this book, that while extreme forms of collaborative models do indeed pose significant difficulties, these difficulties can be ameliorated, if not removed, by careful process design.

For example, the criticism of Fainstein (2000) that an uninvolved facilitator will reduce the opportunity for creative solutions to emerge can be addressed by the planner/expert being a challenger as well as a facilitator, bringing his or her expertise to bear on the process.

In addition, some of the criticisms relate to the scale of the geographic area that collaborative planning is intended to address. The proposal in this publication is for the process to be used in smaller-scale rural communities, which addresses some of these conceptual issues.

Finally, some of the criticisms of a collaborative approach are value-based rather than relating to functional inadequacies. Some critiques are based on the perceptions of those who believe in the primacy and validity of the market and who distrust any process that seeks to make decisions outside and beyond the market.

## CONCLUSION

Collaborative approaches to planning have been widely used, analysed and, indeed, challenged in recent decades. While not without challenge both at the level of theory and in practice, collaborative approaches do offer a mechanism for effecting a more purposeful dialogue between conflicting interests, between participatory and representative forms of Government and between specialists and lay members of a community. Such dialogue surely can be nothing but beneficial provided whatever model is chosen is used honestly and within the boundaries of what is practically achievable.

# 2

# THE KINVARA CASE-STUDY

## *Catherine Corcoran*

This chapter outlines the development of a process of collaborative planning, through a partnership between a local authority and a community in the West of Ireland. The process, which was subsequently called Integrated Area Planning (IAP), offers an opportunity to the parties concerned to develop a shared vision and an agreed set of objectives and actions around local development priorities within a collaborative planning framework. The process offers possibilities for capacity-building of local structures and institutions to enable them to act as effective development agents. A collaborative approach to local planning opens up channels for a more collective community voice about a range of issues and, thus, increased opportunities for wider participation in local governance.

## TIPPERARY INSTITUTE & PARTICIPATORY PLANNING

Tipperary Institute (TI) works with community groups, government agencies and local and national associations involved in rural development in its many aspects. One of the areas of focus for the Institute is in developing partnerships between the various stakeholders involved in land-use and development planning. TI has been involved with a number of communities and local authorities in developing local area plans. From this work, TI began developing a framework for this work (IAP), and sees the development of the framework as a work in progress.

The present working definition used within TI for IAP is that:

'… IAP is an empowering, practical and participatory process to collect, analyse and compile information, while developing the skills and structures needed to prepare and implement an inclusive and multifaceted plan for a defined geographical area.'

TI has developed the following principles to guide the planning process:

◊ **The plan will be developed using an action planning model:** The plan, and the process that will be undertaken to develop the plan, will seek to enable the local community to identify, analyse and address the needs of their community. It will seek to build local capacity and to equip community members with the knowledge, skills and motivation to mobilise community, State and private effort in addressing the development of their area.

◊ **Integrated area planning assumes a commitment to working in an inclusive and participatory way:** The process for developing an integrated area plan will engage actively with all sectors in the local community. The working group leading the process should be diverse, inclusive and committed to a partnership approach to local development.

◊ **The process should take an integrated approach to sustainable planning:** An integrated development plan should incorporate a balance between social, economic and environmental needs and measures. The process will endeavour to ensure that the outcomes are equitable, realistic and sustainable.

◊ **Development plans should be clear and accessible:** The document produced should be written in clear and understandable language. It will present any profile of the area and any results of surveys in full and in summary, with supporting documentation in a format that will facilitate reference, action and evaluation by State agencies, local community and development organisations.

◊ **The planning process should seek to develop structures for implementation:** The process will seek to engage State agencies fully, at local and county level, in inputting to the plan and taking responsibility for relevant parts of its implementation, in partnership with the local community. The planning process should seek to develop clear visions, goals and objectives, with actions clearly linked to the attainment of agreed outcomes.

◊ **The process should be committed to ongoing community communication:** As each stage of the process is advanced, regular communication will be required with the local community and the agencies involved.

**Figure 2.1** outlines the proposed steps to be considered when developing an IAP. All of these stages (except the pre-development phase) were undertaken in Kinvara. Prior to the initiation of the project, the Institute contracted the Department of Food Business & Development at University College Cork (UCC) to conduct an ongoing evaluation of the Kinvara project, as it moved through its various stages of development. Much of the reflective material included in this article is derived from this evaluation.

## Figure 2.1: Proposed Steps in Developing an IAP

| Steps | Elements | Timeframe in Kinvara |
|---|---|---|
| 1.Contracting phase | Contact with the community established and funding arranged. Contract between the Local Authority and Tipperary Institute signed. Seminars held for Council staff. | March 2001-February 2002 |
| 2. Pre-development phase | Key organisations in the area identified. Essential service providers identified. Socio-economic profile conducted and marginalised groups identified. | Not done in Kinvara |
| 3. Data collection | Background data collected. Data about local needs and priorities collected via focus group meetings/other methods. | March-April 2002 |
| 4. Establishment of a steering group | Procedures for group appointment made. Responsibilities defined. Appointment of members, in consultation with community. | April 2002 |
| 5. Capacity-building of the steering group | Group development work. Skills training in communication, networking, action planning, data collection and analysis and planning and environment. | May 2002-April 2003 |

| Steps | Elements | Timeframe in Kinvara |
|---|---|---|
| **6. Establishment of visions and objectives** | Themes based on data collection developed. Ideal scenarios, and practical steps to realise them, documented. Newsletter and public consultation on proposals. | August-November 2002 |
| **7. Establishment of task groups** | Members recruited from the community and statutory agencies. Research on topics carried out. Regular meetings to decide on action points. Feedback and approval by steering group. | November 2002-April 2003 |
| **8. Drafting stage** | Development of proposals in line with national development policies and guidelines. Meetings between steering group members and council officials to finalise/agree proposals. | December 2002-April 2003 |
| **9. Validation** | Publication of the final draft and copies available to the public. Public meetings held, written submissions from residents considered and document amended as appropriate. Report on submissions received and changes recommended. | April 2003 |
| **10. Approval** | Meetings with Galway Co. Council and Kinvara community council to discuss the plan and gain official approval. Plan submitted. | Jan and April 2003 |
| **11. Implementation** | Structures established. Gaining community support and membership of implementation groups. Preparation of Local Area Plan. | Ongoing |

The next part of this chapter describes the various phases within the emerging IAP framework. It outlines the conceptual aspects of the framework to date and examines its practical application in a West of Ireland town.

## STAGES IN DEVELOPING AN IAP FRAMEWORK

### The contracting phase

In November 2000, the Kinvara Community Council approached Galway Co. Council about the need to prepare a development plan for the area. A coastal community and harbour, located 17 miles south of Galway City, Kinvara has become an increasingly attractive area for residential development. Kinvara has always been a market town also and its location on Galway bay has defined its role as a port, a harbour and, more recently, as a tourist centre. It is Galway's gateway to the Burren, which is one of the most important botanical sites in Europe and is of major importance to the cultural and economic life of the town. Despite out-migration, the decline in sea transport and agriculture in the last century, Kinvara turned the tide and has developed as a thriving community. Now, like many towns and villages situated in relatively close proximity to a major city, Kinvara has experienced substantial development pressure over the past few years. This pressure has led to growing concerns over pollution in the bay and the unplanned nature of the housing development in the vicinity. The Kinvara Community Council identified the need to prepare a development plan to manage the increasing pressure for development and to set parameters regarding the level, scale and nature of the development that would take place for the future. Following this, TI was invited to present ideas to the Community Council about options regarding processes of local planning.

In July 2001, having successfully secured funding, Galway Co. Council agreed to proceed with the preparation of an Integrated Area Plan as part of a pilot community planning project. Conscious of the need to adopt a new and innovative approach, Galway Co. Council engaged TI as facilitator for the planning process. Prior to the initiation of the process, the Department of Food Business & Development at University College Cork (UCC) was invited by TI to act as mentors and evaluators of the project and to assist in further developing the IAP framework.

An essential aspect of the project was the involvement of the local authority as the sponsor of the project. This sponsorship came as a result of a progressive realisation on the part of Galway Co. Council that the existing top-down local authority-led system of plan preparation had severe limitations, particularly in the context of the emerging partnership approach to decision-making. In Ireland, as in most other developed countries, the traditional policy-making system is far from adaptive or responsive. Collaborative policy dialogue and collaborative action do not fit readily into the institutional arrangements for public choice and action that exist in most nations and at most levels of government. These arrangements are typically organised around hierarchical bureaucratic agencies, guided by strict mandates and work by applying *a priori* rules (Innes & Booher, 2000, p.18). Collaborative decision-making is not a method to which policy-makers and government agencies are accustomed. It demands that the experts engage with lay people, who challenge analyses and assumptions and use their local knowledge to influence a process that has been granted legitimate status.

Recognising that, without commitment to engagement in the process, the plan would not be implemented and thus would be of limited value, Galway Co. Council was centrally involved in the process. From the outset, the Kinvara project was structured to ensure that maximum learning was achieved internally within the local authority. The following steps were undertaken in this regard:

◊ A Project Management Group was established, involving the Director of Planning & Economic Development, the Director of Community & Enterprise, the Director of Culture & General Services who has responsibility for the electoral area, TI and other planning officials. The role of this group was to initiate and monitor the progress of the project on an ongoing basis.

◊ Two members of staff, one from the Forward Planning section and one from the Community & Enterprise Unit of Galway Co. Council were appointed as members of the community steering group. Both members of staff were involved from the outset in the preparatory planning process and liaised on a regular basis with TI. This was an essential aspect of the IAP process. It is important to acknowledge that the level of personal commitment in terms of time and flexibility demanded by the process was considerable.

◊ Internal training seminars were held for officials within Galway Co. Council, who had a particular remit in local area planning in the Kinvara area. The seminars focused on discussions relating to perceptions of the planning process, understanding the community planning process and gaining agreement of staff to participate in the various task groups.

◊ Elected members of the Council were invited to participate at steering group meetings with the expectation that, through their involvement, they could gain direct experience of community planning processes and methods and thus support the adoption of the plan at Council level and its subsequent implementation. This is essential if a partnership approach is to be developed, as studies show it is not uncommon for elected representatives to feel that their role and position is undermined by the rise of the new participatory emphasis in local governance (Burton, 2003).

◊ Task groups were established to research and to make recommendations around particular topics such as sewerage, traffic and housing. They were made up of community members and staff members from various local authority departments, including those responsible for sanitation, environment, housing, roads, heritage and planning. The groups were involved in drafting objectives and action plans to meet particular identified needs. This collaborative effort was essential in developing a genuine partnership approach. Again, it should be emphasised that this is a time-consuming aspect of IAP and requires significant commitment on the part of the staff involved.

## Data collection

The first activity in the project that directly involved the local population was a baseline study of the existing attitudes and opinions of the people of Kinvara about the priority needs in the community and about their views on the existing decision-making processes and planning procedures of the local authority. It was intended to gather this information, prior to the public announcement and formal initiation of the planning project.

For the purposes of representation, and in order to allow people to contribute, it was proposed that this data was to be gathered using focus group discussions. This involves inviting small groups of people (usually six to 12), who share one particular social or economic feature, to discuss a specific topic in detail. Nine focus group discussions were held in March and April 2002 with people representing a wide cross-section of Kinvara society. One of the surprising aspects of this part of the process was that there was such a convergence of opinion in relation to the principal issues affecting the town and the performance of the local authority. This allowed the facilitators to identify quickly the main issues that needed to be tackled in the plan. At a later stage in the process, task groups were appointed to investigate these issues further, but it was at this stage essentially that the broad issues that underpinned the plan were identified.

## Establishment of the steering group

A major step in the project was the appointment of a steering group for the IAP. The main responsibilities of this group were guiding the IAP process, by developing an overall set of visions for the plan, participating on task groups and ensuring that local people were consulted at all stages in the plan's development. Perhaps the most essential principle adopted by TI and Galway Co. Council in establishing a steering group was that the group be as representative as possible and that all of the different groups within the community would have an opportunity to be represented. This reflects collaborative planning models that call for both diversity and interdependence among stakeholders in any planning process, if the benefits of collaborative dialogue are to be achieved. All stakeholders should be 'at the table' or engaged in some way, if agreements are to be durable and fully-informed (Innes & Booher, 2000, p.7). Healey talks about a dialogical process of mutual learning and allowing for consensus-building in that particular context (Healey, 1997). These writers maintain that stakeholders need to be diverse, if the process is to take full advantage of the creativity that can arise from a wide set of competing interests.

There are choices that may be made when developing a group at local level to guide the local planning process. For example:

◊   An existing group forms the core of the group and then co-opts other people from under-represented groups.

◊   An entirely new group made up of members of different sections of the community, representing all of the groups identified, is established.

In the case of Kinvara, the original sponsoring body for the plan was the Community Council. At meetings between the TI and the Community Council, the latter was very keen to communicate that it felt that it was no longer seen as a very representative group within the area, as most of their members were not originally residents of Kinvara. The Council, therefore, felt it best that a new group be formed to direct the planning process and that this group should emerge from the meeting series.

An interesting point arises in this context about the composition of the steering group and how it is constituted. A balance needs to be achieved between representation of all sections of the community, while also ensuring that existing development groups in the area are enhanced and empowered by the IAP process. Their involvement in the process is vital, if local development efforts are to be sustained and the IAP supported. On the other hand, the IAP process might overwhelm an existing group, as it requires so much work. One of the most important outcomes of the collaborative dialogue, as outlined by Innes & Booher, is that new relationships and social capital are built among players who would not normally talk with one another, much less do so collaboratively. It is also desirable to enable new people who have never been involved in a development group to become involved. Also, all areas and groups need to be included on the steering group. This is a sensitive area and, for this reason, requires careful facilitation.

## Capacity-building of the steering group

Fundamental to the IAP approach is a belief that the process of developing the plan is as important as the plan itself. The actual paper plan is just one side of the coin; the other is developing the capacity of local people to become agents of change in their own local area through their involvement in developing that plan. In Healey's view, spatial planning can help to build up institutional capacity or the quality of relational networks within a locality (Healey, 1997). Various studies undertaken in the UK on community regeneration projects found a clear need for long-term investment in social and community infrastructure and other forms of support, if they are to be successful (cited in Burton, 2003). The methodology adopted, therefore, needs to maximise the opportunity for the group and individuals involved to develop skills that they could use in the future on various groups or committees active in the area. This view is shared by the Planning Officers Society:

'Capacity-building and other support will assist communities in need to influence regeneration initiatives and secure beneficial and sustainable outcomes that address real needs.' (Addison, 2004, p.6)

To address this, TI developed and implemented a detailed programme of group capacity-building. Areas such as communication and networking were an initial focus for group training, with a view to developing the capacity of members to run effective meetings, reach decisions by consensus and operate as an effective unit. This is an essential aspect of collaborative planning, as outlined by the theorists. The group needs to define its own mission, ground rules and tasks (Innes & Booher, 2000). It must create its own tasks and working committees, which have both the interest and the ability to work effectively and make progress. This is what they call 'collaborative dialogue'.

The evaluation of this process in Kinvara by UCC revealed some interesting points. Steering group members reported that, for the first few months, they were not very clear about their role in the process and this took several meetings to evolve. There is a dilemma between spending time on group formation and getting 'stuck in' to the actual task on hand. There was a sense of frustration about the length of time it took the group to form. This was perhaps felt more by people used to working on committees than by those with little experience.

## Establishment of visions and objectives

Following the initial group training exercises, the steering group began the process of developing the plan. The model in development suggested that a strategic approach to planning would start by establishing a broad vision with the group as to the type of place that they would like to live in. This vision development, while informed by the issues identified by the focus groups, was not constrained by the present reality of living in the town but rather demanded of the group that they project into the future and come up with a series of statements that described a shared ideal about the kind of place they wished Kinvara to become in the future. Therefore, it demanded of the group that they put aside current realities and project an ideal future.

The aims of this aspect of the IAP are to:

◊ Create a shared understanding among the group around a set of common priorities.

◊ Create a focus on the broad issues that affect the area.

◊ Provide a context within which development decisions can be examined.

An advantage of taking a vision-led approach is that it serves to move people away from disagreement on small issues and focuses them on the wider picture. This view is in line with guidelines issued by the Planning Officers Society (Addison, 2004), which states that current best practice in planning indicates that planners have a key role in articulating, promoting and leading an agreed vision, making use of integration and collaboration skills to ensure the involvement of communities and partners in the planning process:

'The vision would identify regeneration priorities, objectives, opportunities and drivers, along with an overall approach (*e.g.*, conservation-led).' (Addison, 2004, p.5)

This approach was adopted in Kinvara.

The steering group drew up their vision statements over two meetings. The meetings were facilitated by TI and the statements were drawn up at the meetings, using a PowerPoint presentation, and edited there and then.

If the vision statements within IAP are the core of the plan, then the objectives can be seen as the detail. Objectives are the more specific targets that need to be achieved, if the visions are to be realised. Objectives were also developed by the group and further refined. Actions were allocated to each objective by the task groups established to deal with researching the issues in greater detail.

## Establishment of task groups

One of the most detailed and time-consuming elements of the process, but perhaps the most satisfying for members, was that of working on one of the task groups. These groups were established to develop the detail that was to form the core of the plan. Their task was to take the visions and objectives established by the overall steering group and to propose how these visions and objectives were to be realised. In all, 15 task groups were established at different stages of the process, reflecting the broad range of issues identified at the first public meetings, as well as the information required to complete the statutory aspects of the planning process.

A significant aspect of the workings of these groups was that membership was widened to include members of the community who were not members of the steering group and who had a specific knowledge about or interest in a particular issue. Thus, the members of the education group, for example, included local education providers, parents and a local man who is a vice-Dean of NUIG. The environment and heritage group took on board members of existing local organisations concerned with these issues. This step in the plan may be used as a further opportunity to broaden community 'ownership' of the IAP process. It may also serve to increase local knowledge and awareness of issues and stimulate local debate.

Another vital aspect of the task group membership is that significant players from relevant local authority departments were included as working members of the groups. Three of the task groups were involved in this consultative process. Officials who participated included representatives from the Forward Planning and Development Control sections, Community & Enterprise Unit, Roads & Transportation Services, Housing Services, Environment & Conservation Services and Cultural & General Services. When the task groups made recommendations around particular topics, such as sewerage, traffic etc, they were informed therefore both by local people's knowledge on local conditions and the staff's expertise and experience about the issue concerned.

The groups were involved in drafting objectives and action plans to meet particular needs identified and submitting these for inclusion in the plan. This collaborative effort was essential in developing a partnership approach to local planning, and is very much in line with collaborative planning theory, where the experts engage in dialogue with local citizens.

A significant aspect of this process was the level of learning and sharing of knowledge and information at steering group level. This learning is a crucial aspect of collaborative dialogue (Innes & Booher, 2000). In their research work, Innes & Booher found that learning was not just an individual experience, it was also a joint learning exercise in the successful cases. This was not surprising, as group process and interaction is a recognised way of learning that really engages people. Participants learn, not just from what others say, but also from their own involvement in the task, and because their minds begin to work more actively in the collective effort. In the Kinvara case, the work of each task group was presented at steering group meetings and the content was debated and vetted by everyone present. This also meant that a high level of understanding and commitment to the actual content of the plan was built up. A good level of information-sharing outside the group also took place. Public representatives were invited to participate at crucial points in the process. At all meetings with them, and at other public fora, the information was presented by steering group members themselves, which increased their sense of ownership over the content of the final plan.

While there is some disagreement among the steering group members as to the success of the task groups, there is widespread agreement as to the usefulness of the task group approach in gathering information regarding the different elements/issues that needed to be covered in the development plan. There is also agreement among the steering group that task groups are a convenient means of dividing some of the work of the steering group into more manageable parts.

## Drafting stage

The reports from the various task groups were collated and inputted into a working draft document. In general, the information contained a condensed statement of visions and objectives, along with a series of actions, nominated stakeholders and a time-frame. The task group members themselves did all of this work. At this point, it was believed that the document would benefit from including a policy context, within which strategic issues emerging from the process could be structured. Broad policy statements reflecting government policy and recognised good practice in areas, such as education and housing, were drafted. Guidance on these areas was sought from documents, such as the *National Development Plan* (Department of Finance, 1999) and the draft *County Development Plan* (Galway Co. Council, 2002) to help establish general benchmarks, against which various proposals made by the task groups could be measured. TI and Galway Co. Council staff drafted this part of the document.

Due to time constraints, not all of the task group reports were presented to the steering group. However, at the end of this process, some members of the group complained of 'participation fatigue' and expressed frustration at the length of the process. Participatory processes tend, by their nature, to be lengthy. Any attempt to make the process shorter could compromise the effort to promote greater participation. On reflection, it may have been more participative to ensure that each group was more fully involved and consulted in the drafting stage. Despite this faltering in the operation of the steering group, there was, at the end of this stage of the process, general agreement among the steering group as to its success overall as a working body. For the most part, the steering group acknowledged that, while problems may have arisen towards the end, the body was quite successful, in that it fulfilled its remit of guiding the community to creating a development plan for Kinvara.

## Validation

The purpose of this stage of the plan is to gain public support for, and agreement with, the broad thrust of the IAP. As with the earlier stages of consultation, efforts were made to communicate with all members of the community. A series of meetings was held over three days in April 2003 in Kinvara, in order to present the draft plan to the public and to get verbal feedback. A two-page summary of the plan was distributed by the steering group to every household in the area. Hundreds of draft plans were copied and made available to buy or rent from various outlets in the town. The public was also invited to send in written feedback. The response to this was mixed. Attendance at meetings was not very high, but those who did attend gave detailed feedback. A number of very well-thought-out and comprehensive pieces of written feedback were received and all were published as appendices to the final document.

The evaluation by UCC revealed that public meetings appear to have been very successful in the early stages of the process in generating public interest and participation in the process. The initial public meetings to discuss the issue of planning and to elect a steering group had a high attendance rate. However, as the process developed, this attendance rate was never again reached. Analysis of interviews with steering group members and a number of community members suggests that attempts to encourage community participation were only partially successful, in that, while a number of the community were involved in varying capacities, there were also significant numbers of people in the community who did not participate in the process.

This idea of ensuring an inclusive process relates back to the issues that have been discussed in the preceding pages. The use of focus groups, task groups and public meetings, in this particular project, were successful in getting some members of the community to participate. In addition, the creation of a steering group, which represented as wide a spectrum of the community as possible, also helped in the pursuit of an inclusive process. However, these initiatives did not, on their own, encourage the participation of those members of the community who are more difficult to reach.

From speaking with those who did not get involved in the process, it seems necessary to employ methods that are more tailored to those in the community for whom the thought of participating presents significant challenges (these challenges may range from physical disabilities to transport difficulties, from fear of public engagement to lack of personal social skills, etc). These initiatives may include house meetings and a broader range of communication techniques, including more use of local media. Many of these initiatives may require some degree of capacity-building among the community and represent a significant investment of both time and resources, which as noted above are already limited. It may be that there is a role here for someone from outside the steering group – for example, from the local authority or a facilitating body such as TI – to consider the concept of capacity-building at the pre-process stage.

## Approval stage

In order to complete the circle, the plan needed to have the official approval of two primary stakeholders: Kinvara Community Council and Galway Co. Council. This was achieved by the steering group at meetings with these bodies, where the group formally presented the plan in detail and held a question-and-answer session with both the elected and executive members of Galway Co. Council and the officers of the Community Council.

## Implementation

Kinvara was an unusual case for TI. Many of Kinvara's recent problems were as a result of too much development pressure, due to its proximity to Galway city, and the implications of sudden escalation in demand for housing in the area. This contrasted with issues in other areas, such as Eyrecourt and Hacketstown, where population drift and lack of development were causal factors leading to cumulative decline.

The Kinvara IAP was completed in 2003. Within one year of its completion, the statutory Local Area Plan (LAP) was produced by Galway Co. Council (2004). While the process of developing the LAP followed normal practice, it differed greatly from the norm in terms of content, in that the strategic thrust of the LAP and most of its key elements mirrored the IAP produced and approved by the Kinvara community. This was a very important success and a validation both of the IAP process and of the partnership arrangement between the community and Galway Co. Council.

Despite this, however there were a number of issues that many in the community were concerned about. One interpretation of the LAP that many locals objected to was the fact that the consolidation of the town centre agreed in the IAP was not given precedence over the development of other parts of the town. Another concern was the inclusion in the statutory plan of a proposal to develop a new street in the town, seen by many as unnecessary and not part of any discussions during the IAP process. A major issue for the community was the fact that the amount of land zoned for residential development far exceeded the recommendations implicit in the IAP. This was further compounded when the Council's elected members voted to further increase this zoned area. Many residents, therefore, felt that key issues prioritised in the IAP were not adequately reflected in the LAP, and that certain proposals in the statutory plan mitigated against proposals contained in the IAP. Also, because the LAP contains neither an action plan nor a list of priorities, it remains a set of unco-ordinated aspirations and statements of best practice. Unlike the IAP, it does not clearly define what it is seeking to achieve and, consequently, lacks coherence and prioritisation.

On the other hand, a wide range of actions in specific areas has been identified in the IAP. The defined actions and associated objectives have been categorised into short-, medium- and ongoing/long-term activities. Associated with the activities is a range of stakeholders and agencies, with various responsibilities in relation to the outlined actions. Since the publication of the IAP, the local community has been active on a number of fronts. Major projects, such as plans for a playground and community crèche, the refurbishment of the community centre, the protection of an ancient church and burial ground and a successful campaign to retain and develop secondary education facilities in the town, as well as the achievement of runner-up status in the all-Ireland *Pride of Place* competition, are among the initiatives undertaken. The entire implementation process, however, requires an underpinning commitment by the community, supported by the statutory agencies, to ensure that the spirit and the essential material elements of the plan are realised. This calls for ongoing community mobilisation and continuous inputs from officials in lead agencies.

Galway Co. Council has had a direct and significant input into the preparation of the plan. This input needs to continue through the implementation of many of the elements and to support other aspects. Ongoing support from councillors is required to ensure that estimates are prepared and approved that reflect the various objectives in the plan, and that resources are subsequently allocated. It is also critical that members of the council continue to provide support with the implementation stages of the plan and, in particular, the development of a new sewerage system to sort out the key priority expressed by all groups in the town through the IAP process, which was the sewage in the bay. Until this system is funded and built, the people of Kinvara say that, for them, little will have changed. A plan remains a plan until it is implemented.

## CONCLUSIONS & RECOMMENDATIONS

The Kinvara IAP is an example of a partnership approach to local planning. It was completed by a series of groups made up of members of the local community and from statutory agencies, principally the local authority. The overall process succeeded in producing the plan and in developing relationships between the parties involved. The initial objectives of the project were more or less realised. The process demanded a significant commitment in terms of time and resources from all parties concerned and this commitment was a vital component in ensuring project completion. In its evaluation of the process, UCC concluded that there was a combination of factors necessary for the creation of a more open and complete planning process. In order to maximise public participation in a process, such as that undertaken in the development of the Kinvara IAP, a number of themes require consideration.

## Resources

This case study suggests that, in order to maximise community participation in a process such as this, a significant investment in resources is needed. Merely offering the community the opportunity to participate is not always enough to increase participation rates. In his examination of the constraints facing community groups, Frazer (1996, p.49) maintains that involving local communities in partnerships in a way that is meaningful takes time. Some partners in these processes have been very reluctant to devote the necessary time and resources to empowerment. Promoting participation among the most marginalised in the community requires extra effort. There are numerous causes behind people's unwillingness to participate, ranging from straightforward reasons, such as time constraints, to more complex ones, such as lack of belief in the process or in one's ability to participate. In order to overcome these problems, it is necessary to go out into the community and actively encourage participation through a range of targeted measures. These measures may range from offering alternative times and venues for meetings to capacity-building and training. However, all of these exercises require a significant investment of both time and financial resources. The time commitment made by steering group members in Kinvara was very significant, and the comprehensive nature of the IAP produced reflects this commitment.

The process highlighted the resource limitations under which the different sections of the County Council work. Involvement in a process such as this requires a large amount of time and manpower, which is not always available within the Council. For instance, it has been noted that administration takes up approximately two-thirds of the time spent on this process, yet there were not sufficient resources available for this requirement. In addition, a lot of time is spent working in the community attending meetings, etc. which also puts a significant strain on resources. As such, resource constraints must be recognised when planning how best to become involved in a process such as this.

## Facilitation

The presence of an external facilitator is pivotal to the success of the participatory process. This is particularly so in the initial stages of the process, when the various actors require a mediator through which to come together. This role can evolve as the process develops, ensuring that any communication problems are recognised and dealt with to ensure a fair and balanced process. In addition to fulfilling the role of mediation, an outside body is required to act as a support body, especially for the members of the community who are involved in guiding the process. The complexity of the planning process can often be a considerable barrier to those in the community who may have little or no knowledge of these complexities. The fact that there are unequal power relations between statutory agencies and local communities has to be acknowledged and recognised. The role of facilitator as 'power-broker' may not be inconsiderable in these situations.

A key issue in the process, however, is who owns the process and to whom the facilitator is ultimately answerable. If the local authority is the employer, can the facilitator have the freedom to negotiate processes that may not be in line with what the Council wants? It is perhaps more desirable that the community has a role in selecting the facilitator, who may then be accepted by the contracting agency as having sufficient experience to facilitate the process.

## Communication

The element of communication is fundamental to a successful participatory process. Clear communication is necessary at a number of levels. One of the intentions of the opening up of the planning process is to create improved relationships between the public and local authorities. In order to achieve this, the building of a communication network between both parties is critical if the community is to begin to build a trusting relationship with the local authority. In Frazer's view, the statutory agencies need to build up confidence and trust in the community sector and to learn to respect the different skills, cultures and ways of working and constraints that affect the community sector. Equally, the community sector needs to trust the agencies and move from a confrontational and 'blaming' mode to work towards a shared vision and common objectives (Frazer, 1996, p.51).

Communication between the wider community and bodies such as the steering group, which is responsible for guiding the process, is also key in harnessing the interest of the community. There are any number of existing communication networks that can be used for this purpose – for example, noticeboards, local radio and print media, parish newsletters, existing community clubs and organisations, etc., in addition to holding public meetings. Internal communication – for example, within the local authority or the steering group – is also required, if the participatory process is to be successful.

## Length of process

If a process is to attempt to be as participatory as possible, it is inevitable that it will be a lengthy one. However, the length of a process such as this can often be one of the reasons that prevents people from participating. There is little that can be done about the length of the process, but the frustration with this aspect of the process can be limited somewhat. It is vital that those who are involved in the process, especially those members of the community who may be unfamiliar with this type of situation, are aware from the beginning of the time-scale involved. If participants have prior knowledge of the time factor, they may be less likely to become discouraged by the seemingly slow progress of such a process. In addition, this case study has shown that it is important to get participants actively working on the plan as early as possible in the process.

## Power

In Arnstein's typology, if partnership is to be achieved, it means that power needs to be redistributed through negotiation between citizens and power holders. These two groups must agree to share planning and decision-making responsibilities through structures, such as joint policy boards, planning committees and mechanisms for resolving impasses. In her opinion, however, in most cases where power has come to be shared, it was taken by the citizens, not given by the city. Power had to be wrested by the powerless rather than being offered by the powerful. She maintains that partnership can work most effectively when there is an organised power-base in the community to which the citizen-leaders are accountable and where the group have resources to pay for independent technical advice and support. With these ingredients, citizens have some genuine bargaining power over the outcome of the plan and can approach the agencies with 'hat on head instead of in hand' (Arnstein, 1969, p.222).

For Frazer (1996, p.51), the empowerment of local communities as part of partnership structures is only likely to be meaningful if partnerships themselves have real powers. Where partnerships are *ad hoc* arrangements that statutory agencies can opt into or out of at will, then they will remain unlikely to share any of their power or control over their resources. Thus, those at the centre who hold power must delegate that power to local partnership groups to draw up these integrated plans for their areas. This will mean that those who currently have power and resources are required to share control over them with others. Echoing Arnstein's writing of 30 years' beforehand, Frazer points to the fact that there are still very unequal relationships between the statutory and community sectors. If this power differential is to be addressed within the context of IAP, it will be necessary to provide resources to ensure that there is ongoing training and support available for community representatives in any partnership process. Only in this way are they likely to develop the necessary skills and confidence to participate in the process as equals.

## Structures

O'Neill (1998) maintains that, traditionally, local authorities in Ireland have had a poor relationship with community groups. Even where a local authority has a progressive approach in relation to the consideration of the views of the community on a particular issue or development, in general there are often no structures in place at local level to formally engage communities in policy-making. CWC (2000a) concludes that there are now new or enhanced structures for participation emerging, but they are largely small-scale, explorative and at the lower-end of the decision-making spectrum. There is a failure on the part of local authorities to move beyond rhetoric to action, and to move from *ad hoc* consultation with communities to establishing local policy-making and implementation bodies with decision-making powers and the resources to implement.

In examining community planning in Scotland, Atherton *et al.* (2002) found that there was a need for, and an onus upon, local authorities to build up the infrastructure of the community sector, the local support and umbrella bodies, networks and forums that facilitate groups, organise co-operation amongst them, build up long-term assets and endowments and conduct dialogue between the community sector and the State bodies (Atherton *et al.*, 2002, p.11).

In initiating the IAP process in Kinvara, Galway Co. Council has moved significantly in both facilitating and funding a local group to come up with a development plan for their area. In developing the plan together with the community, the seeds of a partnership approach have been sown. With ongoing commitment by all parties concerned to implementing the agreed plan and the required investment in local community infrastructure and services, an improved quality of life for local residents in Kinvara should result. Linkages to the County Council structure could result in ongoing improved relationships between the community and the local authority. An openness to a move from what O'Neill calls 'abstract physical planning approaches' to 'a more intuitive, flexible and people-centred vocabulary enabling and encouraging participatory decision-making' on planning issues may result (O'Neill, 1998, p.41). The local government reform process, coupled with a more empowered and confident community sector, may offer improved prospects for shared governance and more democratic decision-making on the key issues that affect people in rural Ireland.

# 3

# THE ENVIRONMENT & THE IAP PROCESS

## *Elisha McGrane*

## IAP & ENVIRONMENTAL SUSTAINABILITY

The Integrated Area Plan (IAP) process promoted by Tipperary Institute (TI) is based on a collaborative and participative approach to development. It seeks to address the social, cultural, economic and environmental needs of present and future communities. It seeks to work with communities to help enable them to develop a plan in co-operation with the local authority and other stakeholders, with regard to the sustainable development of their area. However, the actual physical plan is just one of the results of the process. It is also about building capacity within local communities, raising consciousness around environmental and social concerns, forging linkages with key stakeholders and planning for action.

For IAP purposes, 'environment' has a very broad meaning and includes natural and built resources. The geographical focus that IAP employs means that the environment referred to in an IAP is place-specific. The plan is compiled within the context and meaning of the unique natural and built environment that goes to make up the characteristics and features of the rural village or town. Every integrated area plan is unique to the community that participated in the process.

This chapter discusses the role of the IAP process in promoting environmental sustainability within rural communities. It explores the involvement of communities in environmental management within their areas and the input that the IAP process can have in the development of programmes of action and management around environmental issues in a community.

Essentially, the IAP process is a catalyst for a community to commence on a journey of sustainable community development. Unfortunately, there is no quick-fix recipe, or one-size-fits-all solution, to assist the move towards such development. Activities that the environment can sustain, and that a community wants, will differ from community to community. The process is also a dynamic one. A sustainable community is continually adjusting to meet the changing social and economic needs of its members, while conserving and enhancing the environment's capacity to support it. A sustainable community uses resources (both local and imported) to meet current needs, while ensuring that they are also available for future generations. It seeks a better quality of life for all its members, while maintaining and supporting nature's ability to function effectively, by minimising waste, curbing pollution, promoting energy and resource efficiency, enhancing and creating habitats, maintaining water quality and developing local resources to support the local economy.

One of the first steps in the IAP process requires members of the community to reflect on what kind of place they want to live in. On reaching consensus about this, the community then must look at the process involved in achieving this vision. It is often during this initial vision phase that environment-related themes emerge as significant components in community aspirations. Rural communities often define themselves by the type of physical environment they belong to – for example, an agricultural area, a coastal area, a mountainous area, etc. Their sense of identify may be partly based on their physical and functional relationships to other areas and centres of population (commuter town, market town, tourist destination, provider of labour, amenity area). As these relationships are identified, it becomes apparent how significant the environment and physical infrastructure are in how a community defines itself and the future it maps out for itself. For example, does the community want its population to grow, stabilise or reduce? If so, to what extent? Does it want to be a place for people to move into while they work elsewhere? Does it want to become a centre for tourism? Does it want to become a place for industrial development? Does it want to maintain its rurality? All these key questions have implications for the local environment and infrastructure resources.

Key environmental concerns that have tended to emerge in IAP processes to date have been waste management, sewage treatment, housing development, roads, transport, energy, habitat management, landscaping and water quality. In fact, these are usually near the top in terms of local community priorities. When the key concerns have been identified by the community, the IAP process then provides a framework of actions that communities can undertake to improve, enhance and use this environment.

One of the strengths of the IAP process is that it facilitates communities to address environmental concerns in a pro-active way. Often, environmental issues only become prominent in a community in a re-active manner, when a development is proposed that is perceived by the community to have potentially damaging consequences for the area. The IAP process gives communities the opportunity to look at environmental issues before they become problematic. It helps develop consciousness about the intrinsic role that the environment plays in a community's well-being and identity. The process also encourages and fosters co-operation between communities, local authorities and other key agencies with regard to environmental protection.

While IAPs are valuable for a community itself to be involved in, they also provide assistance for those traditionally involved in planning for community development and environmental management. Barrow discusses the need to involve the public in environmental management:

'Environmental problems are often the sum total of individuals' actions, so people may have to change their attitudes to ensure a solution. Working with local people can inform environmental managers of threats, limits and opportunities they might otherwise have missed.' (1999)

This perspective reiterates the importance of a collaborative approach to planning for effective environmental management.

## EU, NATIONAL, REGIONAL & LOCAL POLICY

The rights-based approach that underlies the United Nations Economic Commission for Europe's *Convention on Access to Information, Public Participation in Decision-making & Access to Justice in Environmental Matters* (the Aarhus Convention) (UNECE, 1998) has been a significant influence in the philosophy that has informed TI's approach to IAP. The Aarhus Convention enshrines people's fundamental right to be involved in decisions that will affect their environment in EU and government policy. However, although the Convention was adopted in 1998 at the Fourth Ministerial Conference in the 'Environment for Europe' process, Ireland has yet to ratify it. The main thrust of the obligations contained in the Convention is changing the way that public authorities and bodies perform public administrative functions. The Aarhus Convention is a new kind of environmental agreement. It links environmental rights and human rights and establishes that sustainable development can be achieved only through the involvement of all stakeholders. The Convention requires public agencies to guarantee rights of access to information, public participation in decision-making and access to justice in environmental matters. The Aarhus Convention represents a significant step forward in international law in the area of individual and community involvement in environmental issues. Commenting on it, Kofi Annan, Secretary-General of the United Nations, gives strength and validity to the IAP approach that TI advocates:

> 'Although regional in scope, the significance of the Aarhus Convention is global. It is by far the most impressive elaboration of principle 10 of the Rio Declaration, which stresses the need for citizen's participation in environmental issues and for access to information on the environment held by public authorities. As such, it is the most ambitious venture in the area of environmental democracy so far undertaken under the auspices of the United Nations.' (UNECE, 1998)

These ideas are also reflected in the *Local Agenda 21 Agreement* (United Nations, 1992), which states that people are entitled to a healthy and productive life in harmony with nature and that environmental issues are best handled with the participation of all concerned citizens. It also outlines how peace, development and environmental protection are interdependent and indivisible.

It is interesting to note that the objectives and strategies outlined in the *National Development Plan 2000-2006* (Department of Finance, 1999) make specific reference to economic and employment growth and social inclusion outcomes. There are no equivalent outcomes for protection of the environment. The plan, however, was the subject of a pilot eco-audit, which stated that development would not occur to the detriment of the environment. It also noted that increased investment in economic and social infrastructure, such as sewage and waste management, would facilitate compliance with EU environmental policies.

TI's approach to IAP has a more explicit focus on environmental issues, in the clear belief that they are fundamental to the sustainable development of any community or region. However, that said, there is a move at national level to integrate environmental considerations in a more comprehensive manner. This is in keeping with European and international trends to carry out strategic environmental assessments on National Development Plans.

The Directive 2001/42/EC on the *Assessment of the Effects of Certain Plans & Programmes on the Environment* (European Parliament & Council of the European Union, 2001) was transposed into Irish law in 2004. The objective of the Directive is to contribute to the integration of environmental considerations into the preparation and adoption of plans and programmes, with a view to promoting sustainable development. New planning regulations will require a Strategic Environmental Assessment (SEA) for all regional planning guidelines, development plans and local area plans likely to have significant environmental impacts. An SEA involves the preparation of a report that highlights likely significant environmental effects of implementing a plan. The European Commission has included commitments to the extension of Strategic Environmental Assessments to its own policies and programmes in the Fourth and Fifth Environmental Action Programmes.

Furthermore, sustainable development, and the requirement to take the environment into account in all policies, is now enshrined in the new Article 6 of the EC Amsterdam Treaty, which calls for environmental protection requirements to be integrated into the definition and implementation of other policies, as well as prior environmental assessment of all plans and programmes receiving State aid.

## THE STORY SO FAR – REFLECTIONS ON IAPS

Since 2000, TI has been working with rural communities in the production of integrated area plans. This experience has allowed TI to develop an understanding of the complexities of the overall planning process and how each plan is unique to the community and its particular environment. While the focus and emphasis in any IAP will be determined by the needs of an individual community, frequently it also will encompass sectors required by the statutory local area plans as laid down in the Planning & Development Act 2000.

There are a number of stages involved in an IAP that are discussed in detail in other chapters. Briefly, the stages in an IAP are:

◊ Establishment of a community steering group.

◊ Collection of data.

◊ Establish overall vision, goals and objectives for the community.

◊ Establish task groups.

◊ Set objectives and visions for these functional areas.

◊ Seek validation and approval by the community and external agencies.

◊ Implementation.

There are a number of points during the plan where information is gathered but it is compiled primarily in the initial data collection stage. This can be achieved in a variety of ways, but it is important that it involves the entire community.

In 2004/05, TI worked with the community of Hacketstown, Co. Carlow to develop an IAP. In Hacketstown, a simple form was given to everyone in the village, asking what they liked and disliked about the town and what they would like to see improved. The resulting information then was analysed by the community steering group. The findings of this research gave rise to the main themes for the plan. For Hacketstown, the key areas around the environment were the natural environment, waste management, litter, the built environment and physical infrastructure.

In Eyrecourt, Co. Galway a similar exercise was carried out in 2004. A household survey was conducted, giving rise to the following environment-related themes: housing and infrastructure, sewerage and heritage.

It was clear from this research that issues around environment had strong significance for members of both these communities. It is interesting to note that different communities have highlighted different needs. For example, Kinvara is a community facing considerable development pressures, whereas Eyrecourt and Hacketstown are experiencing population decline and need an impetus of development. By discussing the issues in the context of the plan, they can be examined objectively and in partnership with the local authority.

When key areas are identified, visions are developed, along with objectives and the corresponding actions. Task groups then are formed to undertake this work. Task groups also widen the involvement of the community in the process and encourage people with an interest in a specific area to become involved. An important exercise during this phase is the proofing of objectives and actions against local, regional and national policies to ensure that they are not in conflict. Reference is made to various policies, including the *National Spatial Strategy* (Government of Ireland, 2002), County Development Plan, Regional Waste Management Plan and the *National Biodiversity Plan* (DoAHGI, 2003). At this stage, key stakeholders, such as local authorities, LEADER, County Enterprise Boards, schools and local clubs, also have a significant involvement.

Additional research may be carried out at this point. One such piece of research carried out in Hacketstown was an audit of the built environment. With some assistance and training from TI, a survey was carried out by members of the built environment task group. This survey allowed the group to evaluate the overall condition of buildings in the village and identify the functions of different buildings in the village. It will also act as a benchmark for future changes.

An important part of the process of compiling an IAP must involve the community heightening its awareness about issues, including the local environment. This is carried out through various activities, including research or discussion with experts and other stakeholders. An example of this, which emerged during the Hacketstown IAP, was that the Dereen river is a Special Area of Conservation (SAC), giving it conservation significance at a European level. When the community investigated this further, it was realised that one of the reasons for such a conservation designation was due to the presence of the rare fresh water mussel *(Margaritifera margaritifera)* in the stretch of river that runs through Hacketstown. This has provided the community with new knowledge of a local resource of ecological interest and presents various opportunities for the community to use this information for its benefit.

**Figure 3.1: View over Hacketstown, Co. Carlow**

The people of Hacketstown also acknowledged the valuable contribution that younger members of the community had to make to the future development of the area. With this in mind, a Youth task group was established, to capture these perspectives and ideas. A schools' competition, entitled 'Hacketstown – My Place', also was organised, to encourage students to express their thoughts about Hacketstown, through art or poetry.

Community involvement in the planning process has many important benefits for the community, local authority planners and the actual process itself. One of these benefits is the way in which, sometimes, items are identified that might not be raised by external 'experts'. The following are examples of actions in the Eyrecourt plan around the importance of conserving the local woodlands that illustrate the value of this local knowledge:

◊ 'Re-establish native woodlands and encourage a local rookery back to the area.'

◊ 'Investigate condition of, and seek to protect, the "seven sisters" group of trees, as part of the implementation of the County Tree Survey.'

It is essential for a plan's successful implementation that communities have the involvement and support of external agencies, in particular the local authority, during the IAP process. This is highlighted by the fact that four of the environment-related visions outlined in the Hacketstown IAP require Carlow Co. Council's assistance for implementation. Many of the activities relevant to environmental protection, such as sewage treatment or waste infrastructure, require significant support and funding from the local authority. There is also important learning and understanding to be gained for the community in developing their visions and realising the complexities within which local authorities operate. Sometimes, a community may regard an environmental problem as simple to rectify and may blame an organisation or agency for not finding a quick solution. When a community delves into issues in more detail, as required in the production of an IAP, the difficulties become more apparent. This can help communities understand the complicated environment within which State agencies often have to operate.

It is also important to note that some items identified in an IAP do not require significant financial resources. Rather they require the commitment of the community to implement. Some examples include:

◊ 'Produce a booklet on the heritage of Hacketstown.'

◊ 'Include a green page on a Hacketstown website.'

◊ 'Encourage local schools to get involved in An Taisce's Green Schools Campaign.'

◊ 'Hold an energy awareness campaign.'

◊ 'Organise a public awareness campaign to help people identify how they can minimise, recycle and recover their waste.'

These actions help to demonstrate some of the impacts that communities can have on environmental sustainability in their areas. It is crucial that these ideas are generated by the community for the community rather than by external 'experts'. This gives the ownership of the plan to the community and will increase the likelihood of successful implementation. It also provides the opportunity for communities to take responsibility for their own environment.

An IAP also presents an appropriate context for a community to look at developing guidelines for various activities. For example, local hedgerows have been identified by the *National Biodiversity Plan* (DoAHGI, 2003) as a particularly important type of habitat for protection. A community could undertake to identify local hedgerows and make provision for proper hedgerow management. The development guidelines for issues like landscaping, habitat management and the visual impact of developments can help promote future developments that are in keeping with the overall 'vision' for the area's physical environment. Such guidelines can facilitate the community when it embarks on projects, and may also help individuals or developers in the planning of new buildings or the renovation of old ones. The community of Hacketstown has set out to develop such documents in the shape of a Master Landscaping Plan for the town, as well as a Habitat Management Plan for the area.

The IAP exercise also requires the task groups to put realistic timelines on the implementation of the various actions. **Appendix 1** to this chapter outlines a summary of the environmental visions, objectives and actions that the Hacketstown community agreed to as part of its IAP in 2005.

The IAP process allows communities to look at their environment outside of a confrontational situation. All too often, communities become aware of the need to protect their environment only when they perceive it to be threatened by proposed developments such as roads, landfills, housing or industrial developments. At this stage, communities are reacting to a situation and the 'not-in-my-back-yard' (NIMBY) mentality may develop. When this emerges, it is sometimes difficult then to achieve a resolution that is satisfactory to all parties. However, if a community has undertaken an IAP, it will have a set of visions for the village and the opportunity to reach consensus around how the members of the community see the future of the area evolving. The plan provides the community with a framework with which to approach future development and facilitates a pro-active, rather than a re-active, approach.

The steering group at Kinvara had particular concerns that certain views to, and from, the village should be maintained. These concerns were based on development pressures that the town was experiencing. A task group was established to examine and make recommendations on the issue. The task group conducted a visual and landscape exercise that resulted in certain views being categorised as 'views to be maintained'.

This exercise was undertaken along with a more detailed survey of green areas within the town that were being used for a variety of purposes, mostly passive recreational. Some of the views that the task group recommended for preservation are presented in the following images.

**Figure 3.2: View of Kinvara town, from across the bay (viewed from NE)**

**Figure 3.3: View to SE of Kinvara town, across the bay area**

## FUTURE POSSIBLE DEVELOPMENTS IN THE IAP PROCESS

The following are some suggestions for future IAPs. These would strengthen further the IAP process, the plan and the implementation.

## Proofing

To ensure the sustainability of an IAP, social, economic and environmental proofing of all actions should take place. Each part of the IAP, whether economic, social or environmental, must be congruent. Cross-compliance throughout the plan is crucial. Objectives and policies contained in the plan should be examined to ensure that the economic implications of a plan do not contradict the environmental objectives. Proofing needs to happen, both during the plan-writing stage and during implementation. This process of proofing can be carried out with reference to a multitude of criteria – for example, poverty, disability, equality, biodiversity, etc. Environmental proofing should be undertaken to ensure that environmental considerations are integrated into all policy areas. The kind of community that people want will determine the proofing criteria that are selected. It is important that the proofing criteria that the community select are relevant and relatively easy to measure.

## Monitoring and evaluation of the plan

A system to monitor and evaluate the progress of the plan towards greater levels of sustainability should be put in place as early as possible. Objectives and related indicators need to be identified. It would be useful if communities themselves identified how to measure their position on the road to improved sustainability. When considering indicators, it is worth reflecting on how best to communicate the results to people outside of the immediate steering group, so that everyone will understand the results. It is also important to link any indicators to the objectives that have been set out. When indicators have been selected, there needs to be regular collection of information to measure progress towards reaching objectives. Again, these indicators need to be relevant and measurable. By measuring progress against carefully-selected indicators, the community will be able to see actual results. This may help build confidence and provide inspiration for the group.

Examples of environmental indicators include:

◊  Number of households that compost their organic waste.

◊  Results in the annual *Tidy Towns* competition.

◊  EPA water quality mark for the local river or lake.

◊  Rating from a litter audit.

**Figure 3.4** below illustrates the relationship between a vision, objectives, actions and indicators.

### Figure 3.4: Vision, Objectives, Actions & Indicators for Hacketstown, Co. Carlow

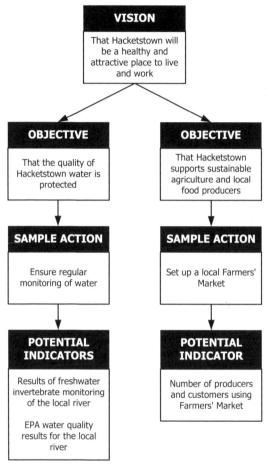

**Source:** Hacketstown IAP, 2004.

## Green mapping

A 'green map' is a locally-created map that highlights the location of environmental resources in an area. The objective of compiling a green map is to allow for a better understanding of existing environmental parameters. Thus, it can help inform future planning and developments.

A green map allows for collective ownership of environmental issues. Green maps involve people in the re-discovery of their local areas and help users understand where their water comes from, where the natural habitats in the area can be found and what they can do to promote a greener, more sustainable way of life. A green map can also help guide tourists to interesting places and successful green initiatives in the area. A green map is a useful resource for a community, to assist in the implementation of an IAP.

# CONCLUSION

All natural resources are interconnected and need to be addressed in an integrated fashion. Each community is unique and has particular issues and solutions related to that area. The geographic focus that the IAP process employs allows for a comprehensive approach to sustainable environmental management, by allowing the identification of priority environmental problems relevant to that area. Many contemporary environmental problems cannot be solved through regulation and legislation alone. By integrating community-led and public agency actions, effective solutions for unique community concerns often can be found.

As well as providing a quality environment for a community, a sustainable environment can also produce many economic opportunities – for example, sustainable tourism activities can be centred around areas of environmental, heritage and cultural significance. Adding value to agricultural and food products, turning wastes into resources (*e.g.*, community composting, anaerobic digestion), increasing community self-reliance (*e.g.*, food and energy production) and sustainable management of natural resources (*e.g.*, eco-tourism, community forestry) are just some of the possible economic benefits that could be derived from the adoption of sustainable development principles. Examining local environmental issues can help develop a 'green' image of an area, so its profile and marketability to potential visitors, tourists and investors can be enhanced.

The IAP process also provides an opportunity to capture valuable knowledge and expertise that may already exist within a community. This knowledge, expertise and sets of skills now have a structured framework in which they can be used for the benefit of the wider community. An example of this might be an individual member of the community who has particular knowledge about the ecology of the area.

They may have records or insights into biological resources that are not officially documented or widely known about. This could provide information or data that the community could put to various uses.

The IAP process can empower a community to take responsibility for its own environment. By looking at the environment through a pro-active window, new opportunities for environmental management can be explored. It may present the opportunity for communities to identify natural resources maybe not previously known about. The integrated approach that IAP encourages allows communities to identify and exploit the intrinsic links between environment, enterprise, tourism, health and quality of life. Essentially, the purpose of an IAP is to enable a community to address issues of sustainability. The natural and built environment has to be an integral part of any community's attempt to address sustainable development. A healthy and clean environment underpins each element of sustainable development, including economic, social and equity considerations. An important objective of facilitating a community through the process of compiling an IAP is that, at the end of the process, there is recognition of the need to treat all the resources in a place – air, water, land and people – as inter-connected, intrinsically linked and interdependent parts of a natural system.

## HACKETSTOWN IAP – EPILOGUE

The Hacketstown Plan was completed in mid-2005. Since the plan was finalised, the community has been actively implementing certain aspects. In physical terms, there is new street furniture and street signage in place and two new playgrounds are almost complete. A new childcare facility is at the planning stage. A new housing estate with 16 houses has been completed, a development of 100 private houses is planned, there are several new buildings in the town and broadband is available through a private company. Composting facilities are now available and the town received the 'Best Endeavour' award for the South East in the 2005 *Tidy Towns* competition. New residents' associations have been set up and a *Foróige* club and a boxing club have been established. The town is receiving more positive media attention than in the past, and people believe that there is a greater sense of pride in the place and a reduction in vandalism and littering.

In 2007, the Local Area Plan for Hacketstown was prepared by Carlow Co. Council (2007). Interestingly, this LAP refers to the IAP in many cases; in fact, the IAP is attached to the LAP as an Appendix. The introductory chapter to the LAP (Carlow Co. Council, 2007, p.15) states:

'The Integrated Area Plan for Hacketstown will provide a basis for the development of a statutory village plan for Hacketstown. It is noted that the degree of overlapping between the Hacketstown IAP and Carlow Co. Council village plan depends on the consideration of the following:

- Statutory requirement considered in the drafting of a village plan, including government policy.

- A village plan must be consistent with the County Development Plan.

- The Planning & Development Act 2000 and the Planning & Development (Amendment) Act 2002 provides the statutory basis for the County Development Plan.'

It remains to be seen how the community reacts to changes proposed in the LAP and how the plan's implementation impacts on the town.

In terms of challenges, the community find it frustrating that no one person in the County Council is dealing with Hacketstown, which makes communication difficult. The flip-side of this is that the Council is probably experiencing similar issues, as it is dealing with different people on different issues from the town. However, the community group agrees that relations with the Council are definitely greatly improved since the IAP process commenced. The task of communicating with organisations and individuals is hugely time-consuming, as is applying for grant aid. In general terms, the community group believe that the training received from TI during the IAP process was excellent. Overall, the feeling from the group is that great progress is being made and that the group is working well together.

# Appendix: Summary of Visions, Objectives & Actions for the Natural Environment from Hacketstown IAP, 2004

| Vision | Objective / Issue | Action / Recommendation |
|---|---|---|
| **That Hacketstown will be a healthy and attractive place to live and work** | That the quality of Hacketstown's air, water, soil and other natural resources are protected. | Major developments in the area carried out in consultation with the community. Ensure no negative environmental effects from new developments. Regular monitoring of water and soil. Create links between local industry and schools. |
| | That Hacketstown supports sustainable agriculture and local food producers. | Research how healthy, locally produced food could be made available to purchase in Hacketstown. |
| | | Set up a Farmers' Market. Ensure that this fits in with County Council landscaper's vision. |
| | | Work with businesses to stock Fair Trade products. |
| | That landscaping throughout the town will be enhanced. | Commission a master landscaping plan, with preference for plants that are native. |
| | | Establish an annual competition to encourage the maintenance of individual houses, housing estates and businesses. |
| | | Establish a Tidy Towns committee. |
| **That local people take pride in their natural environment** | To heighten awareness of Hacketstown's natural environment. | Produce a booklet on the heritage and other interesting features of Hacketstown. |
| | | Organise a series of lectures, nature walks and other activities about the local environment. |
| | To encourage community to be proactive in ensuring a healthy and clean environment. | Develop a 'green page' on Hacketstown website. Provide information to community on how to be proactive about the environment. |
| | | Establish a photographic collection of the area's environment. |
| | | Schools to get involved in An Taisce's Green Schools Programme. |
| **That new developments would enhance Hacketstown's environment** | That any new planning permissions granted would take into consideration the impact of the development on Hacketstown's environment | Ensure that all planning permissions granted would make reference to the town's landscaping plan. |
| | | Smell from factory is managed. |
| | | The potential environmental impact of new developments to be discussed with the local community. |

| Vision | Objective / Issue | Action / Recommendation |
|---|---|---|
| | | That a specification for signage would be drawn up. This is to ensure that all signage for Hacketstown would be of standard format and in keeping with the area. |
| **That natural amenities are enhanced for the benefit of locals and visitors** | That all natural amenities are managed properly | Identify natural habitats in the area. Carry out a vegetation study. Produce a map of habitats. Produce a habitat enhancement plan. Organise training in habitat management. |
| | To improve/establish access to natural amenities in the area. | Investigate public rights of way. Develop access to the River Dereen, the Burrow and Eaglehill. |
| **That Hacketstown embraces environmentally friendly technology** | That opportunities to adopt environmentally sustainable technologies are taken. | Investigate the use of solar power to light the cross on Eagle Hill. |
| | That Hacketstown uses energy more efficiently | That an energy awareness campaign is held. Carry out energy audits of households and key businesses. |
| | That Hacketstown uses water more efficiently | Carry out a water awareness campaign. |
| **That Hacketstown becomes a destination for "eco tourists".** | Tourists to the area will be able to enjoy the natural amenities and make a positive contribution to economy and community. | Develop access to amenities. Produce information boards or signage where appropriate. |
| | | Tourism information on the local environment is produced and made available. |
| | | Meetings are held with local tourism providers to investigate how their products could be made "greener". |

# 4

# THE IAP PROCESS & CAPACITY–BUILDING

## *Michael Ryan*

During the spring of 2003, Tipperary Institute (TI) was contracted by Carlow LEADER to facilitate the development of an Integrated Area Plan (IAP) with the Hacketstown community in the north-east of Co. Carlow. At an early stage in this process, it was decided that a parallel research study would accompany the actual IAP process.

The purpose of this chapter is to report the research findings arising from the development of an IAP in Hacketstown, between May 2003 and April 2005. The focus of this research was on the theme of capacity-building for a steering group.

In summary, the extensive research process suggests that the Tipperary Institute process of Integrated Area Planning significantly develops the capacity of a steering group, across five domains. These domains include competencies and capacities in: *communication, advocacy, technical skills, change agency* and *values awareness*. The research process also documented and verified the emergence of 12 specific capacity-building indicators (CBIs). The central focus of this chapter is:

◊ To describe the research approach adopted, provide an overview of the research context and outline the IAP process adopted in Hacketstown.

◊ To demonstrate how the capacity-building indicators emerged and how improvement across each of them was authenticated.

◊ To outline the "felt" experience of the research participants and give voice to their collective experience as a steering group.

This chapter is presented as a case study that readily acknowledges the uniqueness of the specific research context. Therefore, it does not claim generalisability or wider application of findings. However, it raises some interesting questions for discussion, identifies some themes for further research and, where possible, draws conclusions regarding the TI-IAP process and the capacity-building or otherwise of the Hacketstown steering group.

# THE RESEARCH METHODOLOGY

## Study design

The research design chosen was essentially an 'action research framework', where the action steps of the IAP process and the parallel, but integrated, research process were taking place simultaneously (see **Appendix 1** in this chapter). The research cycle was rooted in 'grounded theory' methodology, where the main capacity-building themes and indicators emerged from the qualitative data collected in the first cycle of research. The second cycle of research attempted to measure the degree of perceived improvement across these indicators throughout the process.

## Action research

Action research can be described as a research framework to bridge the gap between theory and practice. Kurt Lewin, a Prussian psychologist, introduced the term in 1946, when he proposed that advances in social theory and social change might be achieved simultaneously:

> 'No actions without research, no research without action'. (Lewin, 1946)

Action research has been defined as:

> '... systematic reflective inquiry, undertaken by the research participants to change a social situation or improve existing practice, in order to improve effectiveness'. (Carr & Kemmis, 1986)

Action research subsequently has been used in the applied practitioner research settings of education, healthcare and community development, where the objective of improved practice is prioritised.

The characteristics of action research that deemed it appropriate to the TI-IAP research context were:

◊ **It seeks to improve practice through strategic action in a specific context:** The TI -IAP process has been developed over the last five years and the Rural Development Department is continually seeking to refine and improve the process.

◊ **It is a collaborative and participative inquiry, involving ongoing reflection by researcher and co-participants:** Co-participants here include the TI facilitation team and members of the Hacketstown steering group. The values of participation and collaboration are central to the process.

◊ **It seeks to emancipate participants from ineffective practices:** It is the belief of the TI-IAP team that the IAP process has the potential to empower steering group members to become development agents in their own community.

◊ **It is grounded in the culture and values of the research community – where multiple realities are acknowledged and sometimes negotiated:** The TI- IAP process is a framework that is continually adapted and responsive to the needs of a particular community.

◊ **Its methodology usually involves a cycle of steps, including reconnaissance, planning, acting, continual reflecting and evaluation of outcomes:** The TI-IAP process currently involves 10 phases, including cycles that mirror reconnaissance/planning/acting/evaluation (see **Appendix 1**).

## Grounded theory

'Grounded theory' is a methodology, whereby theory is derived from data that is systematically gathered and analysed. It facilitates the emergence or discovery of theory from data, rather than using data to verify an existing or predefined hypotheses. The theory emerges from the data and is organic to the research process. It was initially developed by Glaser & Strauss (1967), but has subsequently become a popular framework for qualitative data gathering and analysis, as outlined by Strauss & Corbin (1998).

A grounded theory methodology was appropriate to this research process because the research question was exploring the relationship between the IAP process and capacity-building for steering group members. If this relationship was a positive one, the process should lead in itself to capacity-building, and the data (assuming that it would be systematically gathered and analysed) should identify evidence of capacity-building, including the identification of capacity-building indicators (CBIs).

## Data gathering

The chief data collection mechanisms were 'user-friendly' questionnaires and focus group discussions, predominantly with the Hacketstown steering group members, the TI facilitation team, and staff from Carlow LEADER and Carlow Co. Council. This process generated a great deal of predominantly qualitative information, insights regarding steering group reactions and responses at different stages of the process.

The chief data collection instruments (questionnaire and focus group discussion) were designed to capture in an incremental way the experience of steering group members, particularly their sense of development or progress and associated challenges with the process. The specific focus of the questionnaires was to identify the skills, competencies, attributes, challenges and training needs of steering group members throughout the process. These questionnaires were repeated at crucial stages of the process. This facilitated the comparison of data sets over time and the monitoring of steering group capacity during the process.

The research did not set out with an explicit pre-defined set of capacity-building indicators in mind but trusted the grounded theory approach of emergent theory, where the theory emerges from the data itself and is therefore intrinsic to the research process and not predetermined by external assumptions and prescriptive criteria.

## Data analysis

An important part of the data analysis process was the identification of themes and issues as they emerged from the data. The identification of themes (such as communication/championing/research and strategic planning/values) was facilitated by a coding process of 'description, analysis and interpretation' (Wolcott, 1994). A grid-sort matrix was then used to quantify the frequency of each theme. This process identified the emergent capacity-building indicators at the end of phase one. In the subsequent phases of data collection and analysis, we attempted to quantify progress across these indicators and compared steering group members' own perceptions of progress with those of the TI facilitation team. In this paper, the voices of the participants are included throughout to authenticate the research process and give due recognition to the values and principles associated with collaborative research.

## Ethical issues

Firstly, it was agreed by the team that we would discuss the research process with the key stakeholders: the newly-elected Hacketstown steering group members and Carlow LEADER, with whom TI had a contract to complete the process. The key motive for the research was made explicit – the continuous improvement imperative associated with our work in TI as a development institute and the desire for dissemination and publication of best practice in a field that is largely unresearched in an Irish context.

Secondly, it was agreed that the research process should not exhaust the community and the IAP process by overwhelming them with additional data gathering and data analysis. The key focus for the Hacketstown community was the completion of a plan and, therefore, the parallel research process would be designed as an integrated and unimposing element throughout.

Thirdly, the emergent research findings were discussed and validated by the steering group members at crucial stages of the data analysis process. The summary findings of the research process were also presented for validation to steering group members.

## Literature

While it is not the remit of this chapter to present a literature review, the IAP process, its guiding philosophy and the focus of this research study occur within the context of participative collaborative planning theory and the theme of civic community and social capital. Some of the seminal theorists of significance to this theme, who continue to influence theory in this emerging field of study include: Arnstein (1969), Putnam

(1994), Curtin (1996), Healey (1997), MacCarthaigh (2003), Taylor (2003), and Humphreys (2005). The work of these authors is referred to elsewhere in this publication, where an analysis of current theory and emerging knowledge in collaborative planning is relevant.

In an Irish context, however, it is unlikely that a similar piece of research has been conducted, given the uniqueness of the TI-IAP process and the particular focus of the research study – that of developing the capacity-building of a steering group members to become a development agent.

## THE RESEARCH FINDINGS

### What do we mean by 'capacity-building'?

The TI-IAP process is philosophically aligned to the values, visions and principles associated with an empowering capacity-building approach: developing individual and collective capabilities to act purposefully for positive change in communities. Its core philosophy is embedded to the values espoused by Taylor, who favoured:

> '... drawing out the unrecognised or dormant potential by enhancing opportunities and access to resources'. (Taylor, 2003)

It was also felt that we needed to research in a specific way the potential impact of the process for steering group members, because an implicit value driving our commitment to the process was a belief around the drawing-out or development of longer-term skills and capacities for the steering group, who would hopefully reinvest this capacity in the community for future years.

Fundamental to the research question, therefore, was the challenge of measurement. How can you assess the capacity-building dimension of the process and the potential of the process to deliver as an agent of development for the future? Can capacity-building criteria or indicators be developed to predict reliably the capacity of the steering group to become a development agent?

### Location and context

Hacketstown, Co. Carlow had suffered a net population decline between 1991, when there were 707 residents, and 2002, when it had fallen to 614.

The decline of its main industrial base in meat-processing during the 1980s and associated out-migration had exacerbated this trend.

Physically, the town had experienced dereliction in buildings and, in some cases, a general malaise in appearance. Following the 1996 census, Hacketstown was identified as one of the five DEDs in Carlow that were classified as most deprived.

At a social and community services level, however, various successful initiatives had occurred in recent years, including the building of a community hall, the establishment of a day care centre, the setting up of a credit union and the launch of a *Healthy Village* pilot scheme. Some of the existing steering group had been actively involved in these initiatives, while others were uninitiated in community development-type initiatives.

**Figure 4.1: Hacketstown, Co. Carlow – Location**

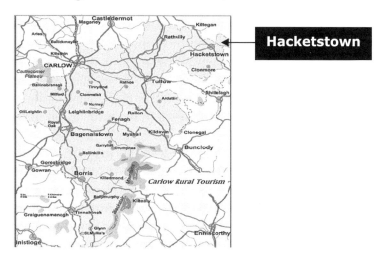

## Profile of the Hacketstown steering group

At the initial stages in the IAP process, a steering group of 22 members, representative of different residential areas, different age groups and different commercial and voluntary sectors of Hacketstown was agreed. While the steering group number was officially 22, it is true to say that the actual number who consistently attended meetings and remained actively involved at a steering group level throughout the process was typically between 14 and 16. The gender ratio was 45% female and 55%

male. The age profiles ranged from 30 to 65 and the occupations represented were predominantly self-employed, semi-skilled, lower middle professional and retired.

## Summary of the TI-IAP process

**Figure 4.2** summarises the different phases associated with the development of an IAP in Hacketstown, Co. Carlow. The research process being reported in this paper begins at the end of phase 3, when the steering group has been initially formed, and concludes at the end of phase 10, when the overall plan is finalised and approved.

### Figure 4.2: Overview of the TI-IAP process in Hacketstown

| Steps | Elements | Timeframe Hacketstown |
|---|---|---|
| **1.Contracting phase** | Contact with the community established and funding arranged. A contract between Carlow LEADER and Tipperary Institute signed. | Jan 2003-April 2003 |
| **2. Pre-development phase** | Key organisations and essential service providers in the area identified. A socio-economic profile conducted. Marginalised groups identified. | Not explicitly completed in Hacketstown initially, but elements of it were incorporated into reconnaissance before phase 3 |
| **3. Establishment of a steering group** | Procedures for group appointment made. Responsibilities defined. Appointment of members, in consultation with community. | May 2003 |
| **4. Data collection** | Background data collected and analysed. Data about local needs and priorities collected via 'H-form surveys'. | Nov - Dec 2003 |
| **5. Capacity building of the steering group** | Group development work. Skills training in communication, networking, action planning, data collection and analysis and planning and environment. | Initial inputs Feb - Mar 2004, but other inputs continued throughout the process |

| Steps | Elements | Timeframe Hacketstown |
|---|---|---|
| **6. Establishment of visions** | Themes based on data collection developed. Ideal scenarios, and practical steps to realise them, documented. Newsletter and public consultation on proposals. | Mar - April 2004 |
| **7. Establishment of task groups** | Members recruited from the community and statutory agencies. Research on topics carried out. Regular meetings to decide objectives and actions. Feedback and approval by steering group | May - July 2004 |
| **8. Drafting stage** | Development of proposals in line with national development policies and guidelines. Meetings between steering group members, Carlow LEADER and Council officials to finalise/agree proposals. | Sept - Oct 2004 Nov - Dec 2004 |
| **9. Validation** | Publication of the final draft and copies available to the public. Public meetings held and written submissions from residents considered and document amended as appropriate. Report on submissions received and recommended changes. | Jan 2005 |
| **10. Approval** | Meetings with Carlow LEADER, County Council officials and Hacketstown steering group to discuss the plan and gain official approval. Plan submitted. | Jan - Feb 2005 |
| **11. Implementation** | Structures established. Gaining community support and membership of implementation groups. Preparation of Local Area Plan. | Ongoing |

## Reporting the research findings

The research findings are reported in three distinct stages:

| Stage 1 | Stage 2 | Stage 3 |
|---|---|---|
| **Development of capacity-building indicators (CBIs)** | **Consolidating CBIs and measuring perceived improvement in capacity-building from beginning to end of the process** | **Checking the reliability of perceived improvement against qualitative data trends emerging throughout** |
| Emergence of draft CBIs from qualitative data collected between stages 3 and 7 of the process | Use of 'self-perception improvement inventory' across agreed indicators after completion of stage 10 | Use of data collected from questionnaires and focus group discussions throughout the process (phases 3-10) |

## RESEARCH FINDINGS FOR STAGE 1

The key function associated with this phase of the IAP process is the *consolidation* of the steering group, regarding its own functioning as a newly-formed group. Its key task during this stage is the gathering of relevant information *via* household surveys and analysis of this data to establish the visions that guide the emerging plan.

At the end of this stage of the IAP process, the research data was beginning to suggest some specific themes that could potentially identify CBIs. However, to ensure a rigorous verification mechanism, all of the qualitative data to date (including data generated by questionnaires and focus group discussions) was collated and analysed using a process of thematic analysis and frequency coding. All responses were now collated and coded. Using a data-sort grid and frequency matrix, the following 12 draft CBIs emerged from the documented responses and experiences of steering group members. Each one is briefly explained in **Figure 4.3** to ensure that the associated meanings are clarified for this particular research context.

## Figure 4.3: Draft Capacity-building Indicators

| Capacity-building Indicator | Explanation | Code |
|---|---|---|
| **Analytical ability** | Understanding cause and effect/problem-solving/making linkages | **AA** |
| **Bringing others on board / social inclusion** | Getting members of the community to support the process and ensuring inclusiveness of all voices | **BB** |
| **Communicating effectively** | Within steering group members and with the community | **CE** |
| **Listening capacity** | To different perspectives of group members and community | **Lis** |
| **Managing meetings** | Capacities associated with chairing/ following agenda/ facilitating discussion and decision-making/adhering to agreed ground rules and distribution and completion of tasks | **MM** |
| **Strategic thinking and planning** | Thinking at a more macro level where inter-connections and helicopter visions enable people to understand and plan for the integrated needs of the community and not just a particular element of those needs | **SP** |
| **Research skills** | Gathering and analysing relevant information to inform planning/decision-making | **RS** |
| **Networking capacity** | Ability to liaise with important stakeholders and to gain support from them for the process | **NC** |
| **Being champions and advocates of the IAP process** | Being able to enthusiastically promote and explain the IAP process to the wider community and external agencies, while also bringing positive energy to the work of the steering group | **CHad** |
| **Positive action or change** | Capacity to bring about positive changes through direct action of the steering group | **PAC** |
| **I can do initiative** | Sense of empowerment felt by members of the steering group, individually and collectively | **ICD** |
| **Accountability to the community** | Awareness and importance of capacity to accurately report and integrate feedback from community into all decision-making | **AC** |

After identification and analysis of these categories by the facilitation team, another indicator was proposed around awareness of sustainability issues. This indicator was deemed to be important, given the values and ethos of sustainability that were being promoted in the IAP process. The TI facilitation team also felt that the sustainability theme would become more apparent for the steering group members as we moved into the more action-planning phase associated with the subsequent task group stage. Therefore the 'Sustainability & Awareness of Issues' (SuA) indicator was officially adopted, although it had not as yet emerged from the existing data.

At this stage in the process, we were satisfied that all these indicators were implicit in our values and expectations. The indicators had emerged organically from the steering group responses to their experience of the process. The ongoing issues and challenges that they had identified all revolved around these indicators. Therefore, the capacity-building indicators were not externally imposed or predetermined. They were intrinsic to the IAP process itself as experienced by the group members. The 12 draft indicators of capacity-building were then agreed (having also been validated by the steering group) as central to the TI model of IAP.

The frequency of these indicators for phase 1 of the process was then established. Each of the indicators has been allocated a letter code, as named in **Figure 4.3**, and identified again in **Figure 4.4**, which plots the frequency of reference for each indicator, as coded from the qualitative data, and presents this data in rank order from highest to lowest reference.

## Figure 4.4: CBIs – Frequency of Reference

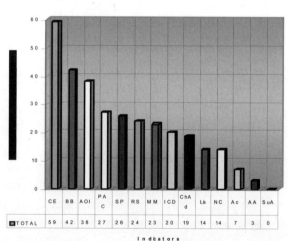

| | CE | BB | AOI | P A C | SP | RS | M M | I C D | ChA d | Lb | NC | Ac | A A | S uA |
|---|---|---|---|---|---|---|---|---|---|---|---|---|---|---|
| TOTAL | 59 | 42 | 38 | 27 | 26 | 24 | 23 | 20 | 19 | 14 | 14 | 7 | 3 | 0 |

Indicators

Collectively, the indicators that had emerged at this stage represent all of the data and the central themes emerging. The total for each indicator as represented in the bar chart represents positive, negative and neutral references associated with that category. The category 'Communicating Effectively' (CE), with the highest frequency of data (59 references), typically included reference to the challenges associated with effective communication within the steering group and externally, but also to the improvement in communication skills after training inputs, etc.

The category AOI (All Other Issues) refers to an amalgam of different issues that included more personal factors experienced by people, such as time and availability, the issue of commitment to a relatively lengthy process, the desire for quality engagement that wasn't consistently possible and other insignificant issues. These issues, while not directly capacity-building indicators in any explicit sense, do relate to the ongoing challenges associated with volunteerism and the pressures of modern living.

Although the emergence of the CBIs vindicates the potential of the IAP process to be one of capacity-building, it does not as yet prove that actual capacity is developed across all the indicators. The discussion will address this issue by analysing a specific measurement of perceived development across each indicator taken at the end of the process.

## RESEARCH FINDINGS FOR STAGE 2

At the end of the IAP process, the indicators were consolidated and amended slightly to reflect the clarification of our own values and the emerging sense of what was important to measure. 'Inclusion of All Voices' was now an official indicator in its own right and the associated indicator of 'Bringing Others on Board' was now included under the 'Championing' indicator. Similarly, 'Accountability to the Community' was now included under 'Communicating with the Group and the Community'.

Having now consolidated the 12 CBIs, the steering group members completed a self-perception improvement inventory. The inventory invited each member to rate their own development across each of the CBIs, by giving themselves a score on this indicator at the beginning of the process and also a score on each indicator at the end of the process (a scale of 1 to 5 was used for each indicator to quantify the perceived improvement, where 5 = maximum improvement). The TI facilitation team members also completed the inventory, giving their perception of the degree of improvement for the steering group. **Figure 4.5**, therefore, allows us to compare the perceptions of the steering group members with those of the facilitation team.

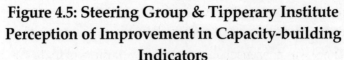

**Figure 4.5: Steering Group & Tipperary Institute Perception of Improvement in Capacity-building Indicators**

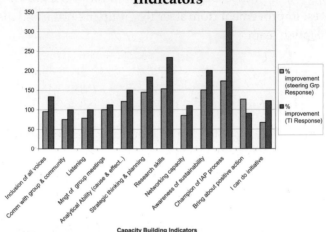

The findings from the self-improvement perception inventory at the end of the process included:

◊ Significant perceived improvement from the beginning of the process to the end of the process, across all CBIs (improvement ranged between 80% and 325% per indicator).

◊ Self-perception at the end of the process suggests that the most substantial improvements were perceived in the following indicators (in rank order): 'Championing', 'Research Skills', 'Strategic Planning' and 'Sustainability Awareness'.

◊ The indicators where perceived improvement was less significant were: 'I Can Do Initiative', 'Networking Capacity', 'Listening' and 'Communication with the Group & the Community'.

◊ The TI facilitation team generally perceived a higher improvement level for the steering group across each indicator than the group did of themselves: the steering group members perceived an improvement rating of at least 100% across seven indicators, whereas the TI facilitation team perceived an improvement of at least 100% across 11 indicators. In addition, the degree of improvement perceived by the TI facilitation team in 'Championing', 'Research Skills' and 'I Can Do Initiative' was much greater than that perceived by the steering group.

◊ There was consensus regarding the indicators of highest and lowest improvement from steering group members and the TI facilitation team.

## RESEARCH FINDINGS FOR STAGE 3

In order to test the validity and reliability of the findings from the perception questionnaire, the discussion of findings now considers the evidence emerging from the qualitative data gathered throughout the process. In other words, was the 'felt experience' throughout each stage of the process reflected in the final perceptions of improvement?

In order to prevent a tedious analysis for each indicator, the discussion clusters the indicators into thematic groupings:

◊ **Communication Indicators:** Communicating Effectively/ Managing Meetings/Listening/Accountability to the Community.

◊ **Advocacy Indicators:** Championing/Advocacy/Networking.

◊ **Technical Skills Indicators:** Strategic Planning/Research Skills/Analytical Ability.

◊ **Change Agent Capacity Indicators:** I Can Do/Positive Action or Change.

◊ **Values Awareness Indicators:** Sustainability/Social Inclusion.

## Cluster 1: Communication Indicators

At the beginning of the process, steering group members were asked the following question:

'If this steering group was to receive some training to help it become a more successful group, what kind of training should this be?'

The purpose of this question was to identify explicitly, and later quantify, the perceived training needs of the group going forward. Their responses included reference to the communication function of the steering group:

> 'Communication skills ... listening ... hearing the views of others ... listening to all opinions ... helping the group work well as a group ... decision-making and compromise ... managing disagreement ... training in how to get tasks done, while remaining on good terms ... seeking advice from other similar groups on lessons learned.'

It was clearly emerging that there was anxiety regarding communication, decision-making processes and managing difference within the group. Part of the TI-IAP process, as currently practiced, includes a phase of focused capacity-building around these particular skills (see phase 5 in **Figure 4.2**). The fact that the group had an awareness of the necessity for skills and capacities in these areas was a promising signal of their desire to become effective in their role.

At the end of stage 1 (eight months later), steering group members were asked to comment on any skills they had developed since joining the steering group. The following responses clearly demonstrate a perceived improvement in the communications cluster, regarding the internal workings of the steering group:

> 'I have become more open and more free to express myself.'

> 'I can explain myself better, I think.'

> 'Feel better about participating in meetings with different people from different backgrounds ... this would be very new to me.'

> 'Communication definitely improved, especially effective meetings.'

> 'I learned about chairing discussions and how procedures are carried out.'

> 'We saw how to run a really effective meeting.'

> 'Our groundrules for meetings were really helpful.

> 'I now have an open mind/willingness to listen and learn.'

> 'We now know how to present information back to the community.'

At this stage, the steering group members also were asked to identify any challenges associated with the process so far, and associated training needs for the future. The responses included reference to the communication indicators, but particularly the external communication domain or communicating outside the steering group. The challenges included:

'Effective PR.'

'How to communicate and deal with people in local authorities and politicians.'

'How to work with the different council bodies.'

'How to be more confident in our own abilities.'

'How to be more assertive.'

'Talking and meeting people.'

'Listening to others outside the steering group with different views.'

'Promoting the process to others not on the steering group.'

'Administering questionnaires to people I didn't know.'

'Dealing with local authority officials.'

'Difficulties with people who don't attend meetings and then don't know what is going on and waste time.'

'Time to attend so many meetings in a short space of time.'

'Going from door-to-door was nerve-racking at the beginning but enjoyable after a while to see how people reacted …'

The perceptions of the TI facilitation team and those of the steering group were similar at this stage, regarding the perceived external communication deficit. These perceptions helped identify further training for steering group members in selected areas, including the need for inputs in external communication, public relations, agreeing communication protocols for official agencies and strategies for networking. These inputs were facilitated at a very basic level before the next stage.

*The task group phase*

As the steering group members entered the task group stage of the process (where they would now be working in smaller groups with non-steering group members from the community, in order to develop visions, objectives and actions around specific themes), there were mixed feelings regarding the communication challenges ahead. Some members were very confident regarding their skills and capacities to manage the external communication dynamic, while others were less so, as indicated by the responses to the following question:

'How do you feel about making contact with external agencies, organisations and State bodies?'

The answers were (number indicates the number of responses for each option): 'confident' (5); 'optimistic' (4); 'excited' (3); 'sceptical' (3); 'anxious' (1); and 'fearful' (1).

There were also concerns about working with new people who were not steering group members. Despite these reservations, however, when asked:

'What skills or qualities are you bringing to the task group phase?'

steering group members responded:

'Being able to really listen to others and see everyone's point of view.'

'Being able to get on with everyone.'

'Ability to speak to local authorities or organisations.'

'How to run effective meetings.'

'Able to get my view across without worrying how it sounds.'

When the steering group members were subsequently asked about perceived challenges for the task group phase, it is interesting to note that only one communication challenge was cited:

'To get my point across'.

This suggests that the communication capacity had improved at this stage, and was no longer a major issue for steering group members.

Members of the TI facilitation team had expressed some concerns during this phase of the process, particularly when some task group meetings consisted of only four or five people and when minutes for meetings were not always recorded. It was also felt that some of the task groups required more assistance at meetings than was originally envisaged. For other task groups, however, there was a much more positive communication dynamic, where meetings were well-structured and minutes accurately recorded. Performance here appeared to depend on the individual capacity of task group co-ordinators around the communication competency. Despite these difficulties, however, each task group managed to complete a consistently detailed report for each theme, outlining visions/objectives/actions and details of relevant agencies for each. Subsequently, it emerged that the task group phase had been a major learning curve for steering group members regarding the communication dynamic:

'We should have had more structured meetings where groundrules were enforced.'

'Steering group members should be more forceful in managing meetings and discussions and leading the agenda.'

'We should have kept formal minutes of every meeting.'

'Participants should be reminded of the importance of their input.'

As the IAP process entered its final phase of validation and approval, a significant communication challenge for the steering group involved the drafting of a detailed report based on the findings from each of the task groups. This report was discussed and approved by the steering group, presented to the community at a meeting for validation, and then discussed with Carlow LEADER and Carlow Co. Council. The ownership of this process was very much that of the steering group, who managed the public meetings and the consultations with Carlow LEADER and Carlow Co. Council. The responsibility for writing the final Hacketstown IAP was fully taken by the steering group members, with minor assistance on editing from the TI facilitation team.

*Summary findings for this cluster*

This discussion of qualitative findings suggests significant improvement in both awareness and actual skill development regarding the capacity of the steering group around essential 'Communication' indicators, while also acknowledging the challenges experienced during the task group phase. The final perception of improvement for this cluster of indicators from the perception questionnaire seems to understate that improvement. However, this final perception rating may reflect a perception that this capacity was already inherent in the group before the process commenced, unlike other capacities that might have been perceived as new and unfamiliar prior to the process.

## Cluster 2: Advocacy indicators

Before we begin a discussion of this indicator, it is important to acknowledge that the impetus for an IAP in Hacketstown did not initially come from the community itself – instead, the town was chosen for an IAP by Carlow LEADER, due to its marginalised status. Therefore, we must examine the extent to which the steering group members took ownership of the process themselves, brought others on board, networked effectively and generally championed the IAP process for Hacketstown itself.

Firstly, we will consider the general championing of the IAP process. At the beginning of the process, the steering group members were asked why they joined the group. Some of the responses relevant to this indicator were:

'To change a stagnant situation.'

'To promote the town.'

'To give something back.'

'Hacketstown has been ignored.'

'To improve the community.'

'To improve the infrastructure of the town.'

'To get a better deal for families and the elderly.'

'Because Tipperary Institute offers new hope.'

'To get everyone behind the plan.'

These responses suggest a clear motivation to bring about positive developments in Hacketstown, and a commitment to the IAP process as a means of achieving this. It became very clear to the TI facilitation team that steering group members had a significant level of commitment to the process as outlined to them.

Towards the end of stage one in the process, steering group members had visited every house in the town to co-ordinate a household survey and were clearly excited about the championing of the process to date and about its potential for the future:

'We are providing focus and direction for the advancement of the community.'

'We are talking for the whole town and people are listening to us.'

'We are clearer in the changes that must happen.'

'We really believe that together we can change things.'

'In working together as a group, being positive and keeping people informed, we can raise the spirits of the community even though there is nothing concrete yet.'

'It gives the hope of better things to come.'

'We have the ability to infect the community enthusiasm.'

'We now have the ability to trust ourselves.'

During this stage, there was also external evidence emerging of improved capacity in the advocacy domain. Officials from Carlow LEADER and Carlow Co. Council (who were interviewed as part of the research process) observed:

'There was a lack of capacity before in Hacketstown structures to deal with complex issues. We can see change now and that the group has taken ownership of the process.' (Carlow Co. Council official)

'They seem very focused ... there is a great spirit ... all listen and all speak ... the hours put into the survey was great ... people work very hard ... individuals seem more confident now ... people seem so proud to be involved ... one of the best groups in Carlow.' (Carlow LEADER official)

'New and more people on board now ... remarkable to have such a big group ... they now value their own opinions ... group development is very high ... I judge process by how strong the group is ... I am very encouraged by it ... LEADER will highlight this as a model of good practice ... very positive in assisting Hacketstown to move forward.' (Carlow LEADER official)

As the group entered the task group phase, there was clearly a sense of empowerment, also witnessed by the TI facilitation team:

'They are capable of so much ... if tools are provided ... can do most things for themselves.'

'The steering group has three to five hugely-committed individuals who are now driving the process ... there is no reluctance to take control.'

'Ownership is strong ... they are bringing commitment and eagerness.'

'They are less cynical about the local authority.'

'They can't contemplate failure.'

There was, however, some concern among the TI team (as the group entered the task group phase) that the very championing of the process and the enthusiasm for action were also potential obstacles. Some steering group members just wanted to bring about change without completing the necessary steps of information-gathering and networking with relevant agencies.

There were definite concerns about the capacity of some steering group members to network effectively and to bring others on board during the task group stage. This has been alluded to in the earlier discussion around communication competencies. The following responses from steering group members, regarding training needs during this phase, acknowledged these anxieties about:

'How to approach groups and organisations.'

'How to liaise with the local authority.'

'How to convince others not on the steering group.'

Steering group members did receive some basic training in these areas and some of the task groups did network quite successfully, as evidenced by the number and extent of agencies contacted throughout the task group phase and listed in Chapter 3 of the final plan. The community and social services task group, for example, convened a very successful meeting of all clubs and societies in the community, at which mutual interests, challenges and opportunities were identified. The task group also collaborated effectively with core agencies in the delivery of healthcare, education, community services, childcare and crime prevention. The visions, objectives and actions for this theme, therefore, are carefully embedded into the relevant resource agencies, and some members of the steering group are now represented on various task groups and fora associated with this theme.

After completion of the task group phase, lessons were learned about networking and bringing others on board:

'I never knew there were so many agencies working in the community.'

'Now I know who to approach.'

'The meeting with CANDO (Carlow Area Network Development Organisation) was amazing.'

'I learned a lot about Hacketstown and problems that I wasn't aware of.'

'A liaison person with the local authority would have been really helpful and saved a lot of time.'

'There is not a bottom-up approach and information was not forthcoming for some parts of our work.'

'It is impossible to get the plan right, if access to key information is denied or just not made easy.'

'You need to be very persistent and the staff keep changing.'

'We needed to keep contacting the task group members to come to meetings … this is tiring but people have to be headhunted … maybe we needed to keep inviting interested members on to the task group and we needed to keep engaging with them … the fact that it was summer didn't help.'

*Summary findings for this cluster*

The qualitative data for this cluster strongly supports the high level of perceived improvement in the championing domain and the sense of ownership taken of the process by the steering group. The TI facilitation team perceived improvement in this CBI as the highest of all at 325%, while the steering group members themselves also rated it as their highest improvement rating at 175%.

While the networking capacity element of this cluster was also deemed to have improved considerably, the level of improvement was not as significant. This seems to be consistent with the trends captured in the qualitative data throughout the process. It is possible also that networking is a social skill related to personality type trait and not easily developed or learned as a competency. The Hacketstown steering group did have two or three individuals who were comfortable networkers, while other members found this capacity a real challenge.

## Cluster 3: Technical Skills indicators

The TI-IAP process is designed to include a substantial process of community information gathering that will guide the emerging plan and actions for the future. One of the first challenges for steering group members is to administer a household survey using a 'H form' and to collate the findings. The survey basically elicits information on likes, dislikes and desired changes for the community. This information is collated and analysed by the steering group, so that community visions are drafted for approval and major themes and issues identified for the task group phase.

In Hacketstown, 428 households were surveyed initially, and 307 responded (72% response rate). Overall visions for the plan were developed from this survey. During the subsequent task group phase, further information around specific themes and issues is collected, analysed and coordinated by steering group members. The objectives and recommendations for the final plan are drafted at this stage.

In December 2003 (eight months into the process), steering group members were asked to identify what skills or qualities they had developed since joining the process. One of the skill sets clearly identified by their responses included:

'An understanding of research methods.'

'Getting the views of as many people as possible.'

'Data collection and doing household surveys.'

'Finding out the main issues for people in the town.'

They were also asked what they had learned about the role of the steering group. Their responses included:

'We have an important research role in the community.'

'We have clearer insights regarding the importance of collecting valuable information from the community and presenting it back at meetings.'

'We can identify the real needs of Hacketstown people.'

'We are clearer on the changes that must happen in Hacketstown.'

The TI steering group members were clearly impressed with the development of group capacity around this cluster of skills:

'The household surveys and the very high response rate were really empowering for the steering group members and the collation of data was a great learning experience for them. They managed this really well.'

None of the steering group had previously been involved in a community survey or the collation and analysis of data. At the end of stage one of the process, the steering group were asked:

'What have you learned so far as a steering group member that could be of benefit to the Hacketstown community?'

The responses included:

'The importance of research, gathering useful information, the need to plan ahead, to source funding availability and to know what we want.'

Subsequently, at the commencement of the task group stage, the steering group members were asked to comment on their understanding of the role of the task group. Again, there was evidence of a very clear understanding of the research and strategic planning role for each task group:

'To gather information and bring it back to the steering group.'

'To find out what the feelings of the people are.'

'To bring as much information as possible to the steering group.'

'To research problems and to help find solutions.'

'To move forward with the visions for the town.'

'To make visions work and see it through to the end.'

'To investigate the key issues and formulate plans for each task group.'

'To come up with a list of things that should be achieved in the area.'

One of the consistent observations of the TI-IAP process is the inevitability of community members becoming actively involved, due to interest in a single issue or specific agenda. In Hacketstown, this 'single issue' theme was also evident, as some steering group members were animated by issues such as derelict buildings and traffic congestion in the town. This preoccupation with single issues seems to dissipate throughout the process, as a more strategic capacity to think in an integrated way emerges. It is likely that there is a clear linkage between the research role in the process and the development of associated 'helicopter' or strategic thinking.

### Summary findings for this cluster

The qualitative data throughout supports the consistently high level of perceived improvement in this cluster. The level of awareness of the importance of gathering information and the sense of improvement in basic research skills was evident throughout.

The qualitative data suggests three key elements that were responsible for the improvement across each of the three indicators within this cluster:

◊   The role of the household survey in helping steering group members to identify and understand the overall issues for the community.

◊ The task group phase and the gathering of detailed information/formulation of objectives and actions for specific themes and issues.

◊ The drafting of the final report, which brings together all the key issues and lays out a cohesive overall plan of action for the next five to 10 years.

Throughout the qualitative data, the references to this cluster of capacity-building indicators are consistent and positive in the perceived learning and skill development of the group.

## Cluster 4: Change Agent capacity indicators

From the outset, it was clear that steering group members committed themselves to the IAP process, because they wished to change and improve the quality of life for themselves and other residents in Hacketstown. Responses to initial questionnaires clearly established this motive:

'To give something back ... change a stagnant situation ... promote the town ... Hacketstown has been ignored for too long ... for the improvement of the community ... improvement of family life ... to get a better deal for the elderly ... to improve the infrastructure of the town.'

Central to the process of capacity-building is the concept of developing individual and collective capability to act purposefully for positive change in communities. Throughout all three stages of the process, there was evidence of increasing confidence by steering group members to take on various tasks and to bring about tangible improvement to the community. Some of this has previously been alluded to, particularly in the discussion of the 'Advocacy' cluster.

*Psychological and practical empowerment*

It is fair to suggest that the change agent capacity – a sense of 'I Can Do' and 'Positive Action' – is both psychological (in that there is a perception of greater personal empowerment) and real, in that members actually see tangible results.

Some of the data collected throughout reflects this psychological sense of empowerment, particularly responses to the question:

'What have you learned from the process that may be of potential benefit to the Hacketstown community?'

Asked at three stages of the process, the responses included:

'We are much more aware now.'

'We know the key issues facing the community.'

'We know how to do research.'

'We know how to communicate with each other and the community.'

'We know how to liaise with the local authority and other agencies.'

'We know how to work with the county councillors.'

'We are much more focused and determined.'

'We are better able to ask for things now.'

'There's a sense of excitement that we are really going to change things.'

'People are talking about the plan.'

'We have the ability to trust ourselves.'

'I now know so much more.'

'People are willing to help themselves if they are shown.'

'I can listen to others that I don't always agree with and respect their point of view.'

'We know how to network and apply for funding.'

The tangible elements of 'I Can Do' and capacity for 'Positive Action' were clearly evident in the following developments that occurred during the development of the plan:

◊ The derelict buildings in the town were cleared and a new housing scheme completed.

◊ Streets and roads were resurfaced.

◊ A new car park was developed, and another one planned.

◊ A landscaping and parking scheme was completed.

◊ A grant of €25,000 was obtained for the development of a playground.

◊ A grant of €48,000 was obtained for an urban renewal scheme.

◊ The steering group elected a new chairperson and brought many new faces to the forefront of development in the town.

◊ The group conducted a household survey of 428 houses.

◊ The group convened several successful community meetings, and produced a number of community newsletters, in addition to various press releases for relevant newspapers.

◊ Over 50 different organisations/agencies were consulted during the process.

◊ Provision made (building secured) for the development of a community crèche and integrated childcare facility.

◊ A member of the group was elected as chair to Carlow Community Network.

In addition to all of these actual changes and achievements, there was the substantial work of developing the actual plan itself and completing a cohesive strategy for the community.

### Summary findings for this cluster

The qualitative findings and tangible evidence from the actual IAP process suggest a much greater level of improvement across this cluster of indicators than that suggested in the self-perception inventory. The perceived improvement for steering group members in the 'I Can Do Initiative' was actually the lowest % improvement at 65%, but received a substantially higher improvement rating from the TI facilitation team at 145%. The level of perceived improvement in 'Bringing about Positive Action' was more positive, however, at 125% for steering group members and possibly underscored by the TI facilitation team at 90% (considering the actual outcomes as outlined above).

## Cluster 5: Values Awareness indicators

'Social Inclusion' and 'Sustainability Awareness' are two important values that guide the TI-IAP process. In the IAP context, social inclusion can be identified as the process that ensures the inclusion of all voices in the development of the plan itself and, similarly, that the needs of the marginalised are fully reflected in the visions, objectives and actions that eventually make up the plan. When the composition of the steering group was being finalised in Hacketstown, there was clear evidence that the composition of the steering group did not include any member of the unemployed or any resident from one of the more socially-disadvantaged housing developments. Although various efforts were made to address this, and two additional members representing residents from marginalised estates did join the group, their participation did not continue.

### Social inclusion and participation

This issue of representation on the steering group is an interesting one and raises more fundamental issues about mechanisms for participation: who doesn't participate in community development initiatives in communities and why not? These issues are raised in relation to rural poor by Curtin (1996) and are also explored in detail in this publication by Kirwan's chapter on the theme of participation (**Chapter 5**).

The TI-IAP process, however, does attempt to ensure that the views of everyone in the community are facilitated and represented. The household survey, community meetings, community newsletters, school-based information campaigns/competitions; and recruitment of individuals during the task group stages are all potential mechanisms for enhanced inclusion of voices and participation in elements of the process.

The qualitative data collected from steering group members during the process contains little reference, however, to the development of social inclusion values or capacities. After the household survey (which was early in the process), however, there was some discussion among steering group members about visiting households in marginalised local authority estates, areas they had never visited previously:

'It was a revelation for me to talk to people in … I have learned a lot from just talking with people door-to-door and I have changed my attitudes on some things ... I never talked to anyone in that estate before ... it is really important that their views are heard.'

*Social inclusion and integration of non-nationals*

During the IAP process, there was some discussion about the possible integration of non-national workers who worked in a local factory. Some steering group members did not see any real need to engage with them, as the majority of them lived in Dublin. Other members were more enthusiastic about encouraging some of them to live locally and to become part of the Hacketstown community. This more inclusive approach was subsequently reflected in some of the visions, objectives and actions written into the actual plan:

'Consult non-nationals about their needs.'

'Organise an awareness campaign.'

'Provide English classes for non-nationals.'

'Ensure that notices of public meetings and community events are available to members of the non national community.

'To celebrate other cultures ... to have multicultural events ... get some non-national members of the community to teach locals about their language, food and music.'

Similarly, the needs of the unemployed, youth, elderly and marginalised are strongly prioritised and articulated in the final visions and objectives of the actual plan but do not appear as frequent reference points for capacity-building during the process.

*Social inclusion and early school-leaving*

One of the other interesting issues to emerge during the process was the issue of early school-leaving and marginalisation of youth issues. While some steering group members were more aware of these than others, the issues were not really acknowledged or confronted collectively by the steering group until an inter-agency meeting (during the task group stage) identified the issue.

This reality surprised some steering group members and became a strong catalyst for the development of strategic objectives in the 'Community & Social Services' theme of the final plan. Many of these strategic objectives relate to integrated provision of services between schools and social services, supports for marginalised families and more pro-active approaches to partnership initiatives between the first- and second-level school sector.

It is possible that this gradual process of increased awareness around social inclusion issues does work at a subconscious level but, in this research process, it is not significantly evident from qualitative data throughout.

*Sustainability awareness*

Sustainability refers to the process of balanced decision-making that strikes an appropriate balance between social, environmental and economic outcomes, without compromising the needs or resources of future generations. Within the IAP process, there is no doubt that this process of balanced decision-making is an ongoing challenge for the community throughout. In Hacketstown, issues such as traffic management, land-use, housing development, enterprise development and social development were all elements in a community planning process, where lack of development rather than excessive development was the reality.

In this context, the pressures for sustainable planning are different to those typically experienced in a community, where the challenge is to halt the pace of development. Nonetheless, it is clear from the visions, objectives and actions of the final Hacketstown plan that the sustainability imperative is embedded right across the major themes of 'Arts & Heritage', 'Built Environment', 'Business & Employment', 'Community & Social Services', 'Crime & Security', 'Environment', 'Physical Infrastructure', 'Tourism', 'Traffic Management' and 'Litter & Waste Management'.

The following are examples of objectives from the plan that embody this awareness of the values associated with sustainability:

'That the scale and pace of development be evenly matched over the next 10 years.'

'That green areas and landscaping are included in all new developments.'

'That everyone working in Hacketstown is able to find suitable housing to buy or rent.'

'That suitable and appropriate enterprises will be investigated to locate in Hacketstown.'

'That "shop local" campaigns are developed and local businesses supported.'

'That all senior citizens and people with special needs who wish to live in Hacketstown be supported in their own environment.'

'That a modern integrated health service be available to everyone in the town.'

'That all residents are included and invited to participate fully in community groups and activities.'

'That we ... create activities that attract young people away from alcohol/drug abuse and vandalism.'

'That the quality of Hacketstown's air, water, soil and other natural resources are protected.'

'That Hacketstown supports sustainable agriculture and local food producers.'

### Summary findings for this cluster

It is interesting that there is little reference to the sustainability or social inclusion issues (or associated values) in much of the qualitative data gathered during the process but yet the visions, objectives and actions of the final plan reflect strong sustainability and social inclusion values. The subtle insistence by the TI facilitation team in helping the steering group to value proof the final plan is possibly responsible for this.

Throughout the IAP process, however, the steering group members are exposed to various inputs, discussions and experiences that potentially raise awareness of these values. It is the opinion of the TI facilitation team, however, that these values need to be made much more explicit in the process itself and need to be embedded in the hearts and minds of the steering group participants.

The level of perceived improvement regarding 'Sustainability Awareness' for the steering group at the end of the process was very positive at 150% (steering group rating) and 250% (TI team rating); 'Social Inclusion' was 95% and 175% respectively. This latter TI rating possibly overstates what was observed and felt throughout the process regarding the actualization of this indicator.

## Overall summary of significant research findings

The research findings may be summarised as:

◊ The research process suggests that the TI-IAP process did develop the capacity of the Hacketstown steering group members to become a potential development agent.

◊ Experience of the TI-IAP process yielded 12 specific capacity-building indicators – the majority of which emerged organically from the data. This suggests that the process itself is intrinsically one of capacity-building.

◊ Significant improvement was registered across each of the indicators, as perceived by steering group members themselves and the TI facilitation team.

◊ Data collected throughout the process (which documents incrementally the felt experience of improvement in capacity-building by steering group members) is largely consistent with overall perceived improvement at the end of the process. Each steering group member used the 'self-perception improvement inventory' to quantify their overall progress across each capacity-building indicator.

◊ There is some inconsistency between data sets regarding the level of improvement felt in the values indicators, especially the 'Sustainability' and 'Social Inclusion' indicators. While the visions, objectives and actions of the final plan suggest that these values were present throughout, the qualitative data does not corroborate this.

◊ Qualitative data collected throughout also suggests that more capacity was developed in the 'Communication' and 'I Can Do' indicators than implied in the final perception measurement.

◊ Self-perception of improvement at the end of the process suggests that the greatest improvement in capacity-building was in indicators largely unfamiliar to the steering group prior to this process: 'Championing the IAP Process', 'Strategic Thinking & Planning', 'Research Skills' and 'Sustainability Awareness'. This might imply that steering group members were starting from a low base of expertise or familiarity with these indicators, whereas a perception of latent capacity could have influenced a lower improvement scoring in familiar indicators such as 'Communication', 'I Can Do' and 'Networking'.

◊   Qualitative data collected at the very end of the process implies a definite sense of capacity-building for the steering group and is possibly a richer source of insight than the more quantitative indicator measurement. A sample of this data will now be presented.

At the very end of the TI-IAP process, steering group members were very enthusiastic about remaining with the process for the implementation stage – demonstrating an ownership of the process and a confidence to implement the plan:

'I will remain on, as I am eager to see us move forward.'

'I wish to contribute to the ongoing development plan.'

'To see the visions become a reality.'

'I have come this far and I want to see it through as I have become more active in the town.'

'I will remain because I know we will achieve our aim.'

'Yes, we are in a much stronger position now to make it happen.'

'I will stay as this is a really good group for the town and we have already achieved so much.'

Equally, there was an impressive sense of reality about the need to liaise appropriately with the local authority and other agencies, so that ongoing resources would be accessed:

'The group will now communicate with the Council in a rational manner and will achieve in the long run.'

'We have a lot more knowledge and "know-how" for dealing with officials and situations.'

'We will continue talking to the relevant groups and make the town plan more important to Carlow Co. Council.'

'We will be more assertive about what we want from the local authority.'

'I fear that left to their own devices the council will give us lip-service.'

The group were also clear on the characteristics they required as a group for the future:

> 'Determination … energy … vision … remain focused … working together to achieve vision … communicating with all members of the steering group … attend meetings, obey the ground rules and put in the work … communicate with the Co. Council and local community … tenacity, consistency and leadership … we need to work firmly together … we need to keep thinking strategically.'

And finally, did the steering group members think that the TI-IAP process developed their potential to contribute to the future of Hacketstown? Their responses were:

> 'Yes, absolutely.'

> 'Helped the group stay together, which would not have happened otherwise.'

> 'Provided a role model for us of how we should do our business as a group.'

> 'Provided us with a stable group dynamic for the future.'

> 'Gave us the insight and explained over time how to proceed and guidelines on how to implement the plan.'

> 'Yes, absolutely … without them it would not have happened.'

> 'Yes, they gave us a step-by-step guide to make the plan come together.'

> 'They showed us how to gather information.'

> 'Yes, the groundrules for meetings were excellent.'

> 'The contacts we made with councillors/local groups.'

> 'We have learnt a lot from good time management at meetings.'

> 'Yes, we have structure, a fresh-faced group, a methodology and our confidence has improved.'

> 'Yes, it helped us see the overall picture and how to relate the different strategies needed to get things done.'

> 'Yes, it made a huge contribution: the three big contributions were the effective running of meetings, the gathering of information and improved ways of dealing with the local authority.'

The TI facilitation team's responses to the same question were:

'Yes, it challenged the group to develop effective mechanisms for meetings and decision-making.'

'Forced the group to challenge some long-held biases.'

'Helped the group to network properly.'

'Challenged existing power-holders and revitalised a community structure.'

'Empowered members to speak for, and to, a community.'

'Essential communication skills, such as presentation skills and report-writing, were developed for some members.'

'It gave them a roadmap for a comprehensive consultation and collaborative process that delivered a plan for their community.'

'It gave a focus and a big-picture strategic approach to a group (some of whom were caught up in single issue thinking).'

'Helped them become politically aware in a positive way regarding effective networking, lobbying and accessing resources (*e.g.*, funding allocations).'

'Something about the process and developing a pride of place that cannot be easily measured.'

'They observed the TI facilitation approach where "walking the walk" was instrumental in their own capacity-building.'

'The entire process opened their eyes to the whole range of agencies and Government Departments that have a stake in their community. These agencies are now seen as resources to call on and not viewed in a negative way. I think this is really important.'

'This group can never be the same again and the fact that the members of the steering group are all staying involved for the implementation says something about their self-confidence for the future.'

'I think those who were on the steering group with a business hat have radically changed some of their thinking about social exclusion issues due to the process.'

## ISSUES IDENTIFIED FOR FURTHER RESEARCH

These include:

◊ **Does the profile of the steering group significantly affect the research outcomes?** It is likely that the profile of the steering group does impact significantly on the research findings. The Hacketstown steering group were very task-focused, similarly motivated regarding the development imperative for an area of economic decline, largely non-conflictual in their approach and slightly biased in representation of the small business sector. A profile of the group using the Meredith Belbin team role inventory (Belbin, 1988) partially confirms this. More than half of the group were profiled as either 'teamworkers' or 'implementers', while only 7% were categorised as 'resource investigators', which is compatible with the challenge of networking and external communication experienced throughout some of the process. However, it is difficult to be conclusive about this, in the absence of a further research process that would facilitate comparison with a different steering group.

◊ **Are the 12 capacity-building indicators reliable predictors of change capacity for the future in Hacketstown?** This is a very relevant question, as the scope of the research could not include the implementation phase. Some of the omens are very positive, but they cannot guarantee successful outcomes. All of the steering group members have remained on the steering committee to oversee the implementation phase and have identified a very positive list of criteria necessary for successful implementation of the plan including appropriate structures, an annual action plan, retention of task groups, provision of training in plan development and implementation, support from a community development specialist, co-operation of the local authority and other State sector agencies, effective communication with the community and plans for the development of a community fund. Throughout the Hacketstown process, it was felt that the importance of support from the local authority, LEADER and other State agencies is crucial to every stage of the process. The future success of the implementation phase is particularly dependent on this support from the State sector. There are, therefore, many external factors that can challenge the capacity of the steering group to be an ongoing development agent. However, it would require another research cycle to address the longer-term findings in this regard.

◊ **Are any of the research findings transferable or does the context localise the findings?** It is likely that the current TI-IAP process would yield similar capacity-building indicators in other locations, and it is also possible that progress would be made across many of these indicators. It is likely, however, that the local context, the socio-economic status of the local development agenda and the steering group profile would each have a significant bearing on how these indicators would be experienced by the research participants.

*Challenges identified*

The findings are all based on the unique challenges associated with the specific context of the research setting in Hacketstown. The overall findings should perhaps also be considered against the following challenges to the capacity-building process, identified by the TI facilitation team as they reviewed the experience:

◊ Practicalities concerning the geographical distance from Hacketstown for TI personnel and the limited time available to invest in the process.

◊ The profile of Hacketstown as a peripheral community meant it started from a low infrastructural base.

◊ Difficulties of breaking through existing norms around social exclusion issues.

◊ Low level of local authority involvement for much of the process.

◊ Over-reliance on LEADER as a local support agent.

◊ Lack of representation from local authority housing estates.

◊ Low level of awareness and capacity to deal with planning issues.

◊ Inability to respond to *all* the training needs of the group (due to time/distance/finance).

◊ Need for a more intensive and focused period of capacity-building, particularly before the 'task group' phase.

◊ Hesitancy of steering group members to declare all the 'beneath the surface issues' (the learning here for TI is to legitimise openness at a very early stage in the process).

◊ Absence of youth voice on the steering group.

◊ Legacy of old attitudes, particularly the negative one towards the local authority.

◊ Infrequent attendance by a small number of committee members, whose lack of information sometimes required a recycling of previous discussions.

## CONCLUSION

Throughout the IAP process in Hacketstown, the research evidence suggests that the TI approach does draw out unrecognised or dormant potential by enhancing opportunities and access to resources. In so doing, it has the capacity to develop the individual and collective capabilities of a steering group to act purposefully for positive change in their own community. The integrated area planning process was experienced by the Hacketstown steering group as a significantly positive one, as reported in the research findings.

The process itself generated 12 capacity-building indicators that suggest the inherent and intrinsic nature of the process to enhance capacity-building for steering group members. Significant improvement was verified across each of these indicators throughout the process. The quantitative measurement of perceived improvement, taken at the end of the process, was verified and checked against qualitative data collected throughout the research process. This data substantially corroborated the positive findings and, despite the challenges experienced, suggests that the TI-IAP process does develop the capacity of steering group members to become development agents.

# Appendix: TI Research Timetable for the Hacketstown IAP Process

| Date | Data Collection method | Focus |
|---|---|---|
| **20 May 2003** | TI team meeting | General research discussion/identifying the focus. |
| **26 May 2003** | Hacketstown steering group initial questionnaire | To establish skills/fears/training needs. |
| **Dec 2003** | Hacketstown steering group interim questionnaire | To document reactions to date and possible changes in perceptions since first questionnaire. |
| **Dec 2003** | Steering Group Belbin profile | To provide some insight into the overall group type profile and presence of functional roles. |
| **28 Jan 2004** | Interviews with G. Deering, Carlow Co. Council, and Mary Walsh, Carlow LEADER | To establish the views of these key stakeholders about the process to date and to act as an indicator of progress. |
| **2 Feb 2004** | Focus group discussion with steering group members | To seek further clarification of issues raised in interim questionnaire and identify emerging issues. |
| **4 Feb 2004** | TI team interim questionnaire and group discussion | To establish the perceptions of TI team regarding aspects of the process – for example, the steering group and issues emerging at this stage of the process. |
| **10 May 2004** | Initial survey of task group members and focus group discussion | To establish perceptions of skills/qualities at this action stage of the process. |
| **July 2004** | As above, end of task group | To monitor skill development at the end of the task group phase. |
| **7 Feb 2005** | End of process review steering group questionnaire & group discussion | To compare overall self-perception of skill levels from the beginning of the process to the end. To assess the overall process as experienced by the steering group members. To assess the perceptions of group members going forward to the implementation stage. |
| **August 2005** | Post-launch and discussion with steering group members | To present initial research findings to the steering group and validate/amend the key findings as appropriate. |

# 5

# EXPLORING THE CAPACITY OF INDIVIDUALS TO PARTICIPATE

## *Bridget Kirwan*

In the context of the Integrated Area Planning (IAP) process, as described earlier, one of the key elements of the process is the participation of the various stakeholders at all stages. The term 'participation' has been widely used in this context, but the implications of the term, both for those who facilitate and for the stakeholders whose plan it is intended to be, are not well understood. This chapter explores the challenge this presents and, in particular, focuses on the factors that impact on the capacity of the individual to participate in the process.

The chapter first explores the various definitions and concepts associated with the term participation, with a view to establishing a definition that can reasonably be used by those seeking 'participation' in the IAP process. It then goes on to explore some of the challenges that arise in the search for effective participation. To this end, the chapter attempts to bring some of what we know about human development to bear on what we know about participation in this context.

The paper also explores our understanding of group participation and how this influences the individual's choice to participate. It then proceeds to examine why the experience of group process is successful for some and unsatisfactory for others. The chapter uses data that emerged from a variety of IAP plans facilitated by Tipperary Institute (TI) to highlight some of the emerging data. In concluding, the chapter makes key recommendations for those who want to develop the IAP process and to share the learning from the experience, in a way that benefits all those who facilitate and participate in such processes.

## DEFINING PARTICIPATION

In setting out the parameters of this chapter, it is essential to define what is meant by the term 'participation':

> 'Participation is the process through which stakeholders influence and share control over priority-setting, policy-making, resource allocations and access to public goods and services. (Kende-Robb, 2005).

This definition gives rise to other issues that require consideration. Is the concept of participation to be considered to be equivalent to 'involvement', which can be defined simultaneously as 'to include or contain as a necessary part' and 'to make complicated; tangle'.

In turn, what might we understand by the term 'to take part', and is the implication of this term different, when contrasted with to 'become actively involved'? Does 'to take part' imply that there is a level of attendance and 'become actively involved' mean that the participant takes responsibility for the event or process? What then would we understand by the phrase to 'share in'? Does that imply a level of sharing of the inputs and the outputs from the project? Is there a difference between the concept 'to participate' and the process we might call 'participation'?

The following extract from the *Washington Post* (23 November 2005) illustrates the dilemma:

> '"What we simply determined was that the definition of 'participation' was something litigated, and what the court concluded was that attending meetings, and even making presentations, did not rise to the level of fully participating", Funk said.

> 'Lautenberg sees it differently … (he) said that, when he asked the question, he was thinking of the word "participation" in broad terms. Here's his definition: "If you're doing anything more than breathing in the room when you're there. Even if you're a silent observer."'

In considering this dilemma, it appears that the definitions of participation are also context-dependant. The concept of participation has been adopted at many levels and in different spheres. Politicians seek to have groups 'participate in the process', organisations want employees to 'actively participate at work', trainers want clients to 'participate' in the programme and we have 'participatory processes' for the development of strategies for communities and organisations. Experience suggests that, while the terms used are the same, the meaning is not.

Some of the variation comes from different concepts related to what might be described as levels of participation. Arnstein's model of participation, referred to in earlier chapters, refers to the 'ladder of participation'. The model below shows how this might be represented from a practical perspective; it suggests that the version of 'participation' that is subscribed to determines both the desired outcomes and the processes that will enable these outcomes to be achieved.

## Figure 5.1: Participation

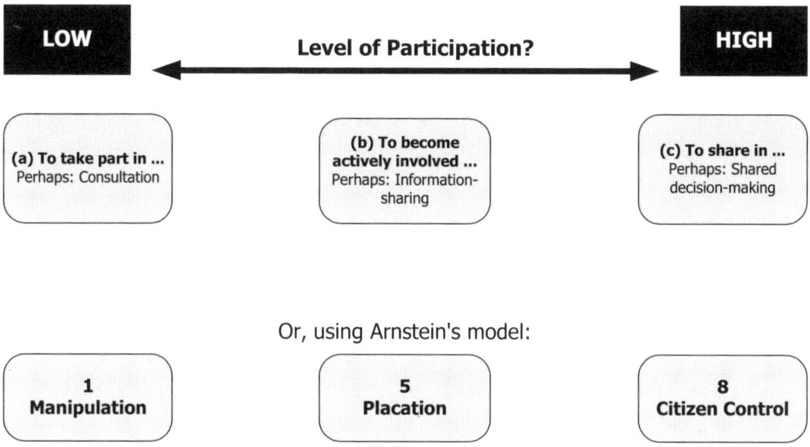

| LOW | Level of Participation? | HIGH |
| --- | --- | --- |
| (a) To take part in ... Perhaps: Consultation | (b) To become actively involved ... Perhaps: Information-sharing | (c) To share in ... Perhaps: Shared decision-making |

Or, using Arnstein's model:

| 1 Manipulation | 5 Placation | 8 Citizen Control |
| --- | --- | --- |

Source: Adaptation by author.

Some of the characteristics of this view of participation suggest that, at Low levels, for example, people will attend meetings (point (a) above), will actively speak or become involved with the discussion at the meeting (point (b) above) and will take ownership for the tasks that might need to be completed to achieve the objectives of group (point (c) above).

The thinking around this is reflected in the following model, taken from a training model that focuses on working with young people. The model introduces the relationship between the power of the youth worker and the power of the young people. It identifies various models of involvement, and marks the place where this power is shared between the youth worker and the young people, identifying it as 'participation'.

### Figure 5.2: Power & Involvement

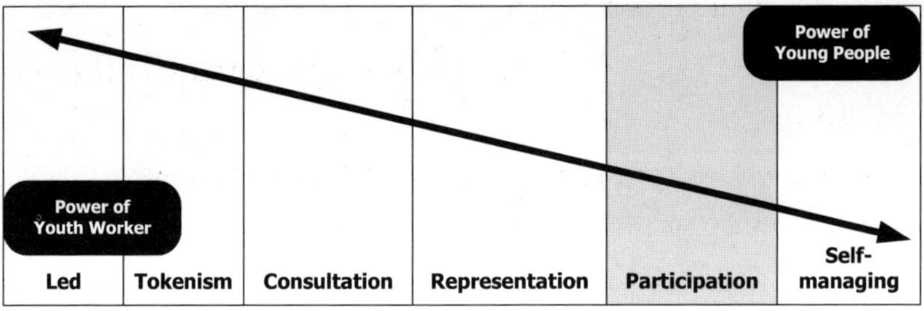

This dilemma is mirrored in this extract from the Community Workers Co-operative, Galway, which states:

> '… full participation can be usefully contrasted with other degrees of participation. At the other end of the spectrum is what might be called "pseudo-participation", where people are consulted and given the impression of involvement, but have no real influence over decisions. Then there are various degrees of "partial participation", in which people have some influence but not a determining voice. In a system of full participation, the citizens or members of some other organisation have full control over decision-making.' (CWC, 1997, p.12)

The philosopher Rousseau (1712-1778) suggested that the purpose of participation was three-fold:

◊ It increases the value of his freedom to the individual.

◊ Ensures that no person can be master of any other and enables laws created collectively, therefore, to be more readily accepted by the whole group.

◊ It also acts to integrate the person into the community, by increasing their sense of belongingness.

The fundamental problem of all social organisation, therefore, is to secure the participation of every individual in the general will. The need for individual participation is driven by a number of different agendas: the most significant in the context of the IAP process is the demands of a democratic context.

A community development perspective suggests the following purposes for ensuring participation:

> 'Participation as a tool in **developing equality** between peoples ...'
>
> 'Participation as a tool in enabling individuals to exercise their **own autonomy/self-determination**.'
>
> 'Participation as a tool in the **development of the concept and practice of community**.'
>
> '**Self-development:** The idea here is that, by fully participating in decision-making, people develop themselves as human beings and as citizens. They learn new skills, expand their knowledge of the world, develop their relationships with others, and generally expand their horizons. Participatory democracy is an area of personal growth and fulfilment.' (CWC, 1997, p.13)

Research from a sustainable development perspective suggests that:

> 'Broad participation helps to open up a debate to new ideas and sources of information; expose issues that need to be addressed; enable problems, needs and preferences to be expressed; identify the capabilities required to address them; and develop consensus on the need for action that leads to better implementation. Central government must be involved (providing leadership, shaping incentive structures and allocating financial resources) but multistakeholder processes are also required, involving decentralised authorities, the private sector and civil society, as well as marginalized groups. This requires good communication and information mechanisms with a premium on transparency and accountability.' (Dalal-Clayton & Bass, 2002, p.34).

From the perspective of work organisations, where much current research in participation has come, the search for increased productivity there has motivated an exploration of a variety of methods of organising work to increase the participation levels of workers.

One of these methods is 'participative decision-making' (PDM), which, it is argued:

'... increases employee involvement in how task characteristics are operationalised; for example, PDM mediates the influence of autonomy on satisfaction and commitment (Mueller *et al.*, 1999). Similarly, Zeffane (1994) found that increased variety achieved through PDM increased job satisfaction. Employee PDM decreases role ambiguity and conflict and increases knowledge of results, so uncertainty is reduced, and this, in turn, provides motivational benefits that improve performance (Degeling *et al.*, 2000; Healy & McKay, 2000). Further, such involvement gives decisions greater meaning to employees and supports work being "... purposeful and meaningful" (Knoop, 1991, p. 776), so consequently employees are more willing to expend effort. Subsequently, the sense of control and worth employees experience promotes further involvement (Brown, 1996), benefiting performance, satisfaction and, ultimately, commitment (Allen & Meyer, 1990; Meyer *et al.*, 1993).' (Scott-Ladd & Marshall, 2004, p.1)

The interest in the issue of participation, therefore, has been of interest for a variety of disciplines, since it has implications for the individual and for the society to which he belongs. It has both process and outcome implications, in that it is concerned both with how decisions are made and the purpose for which these decisions are made. It is concerned with the short- and long-term implications of the presence or absence of participation for the 'good' of society as a whole.

In the context of this chapter, these perspectives contribute to the creation of an environment that influences the choice and the ability of the individual to participate in any given process or not.

The focus of this chapter is to explore what issues influence an individual's propensity to participate in a participatory planning process and what we might learn from this that has implications for the implementation of the IAP process.

## THE INDIVIDUAL'S MOTIVATION TO PARTICIPATE

In exploring the issue of individual propensity to participate, the discussion has been influenced by perspectives from social psychology and developmental psychology, which might inform our thinking on the issues surrounding the motivation of individuals to participate. This section looks at different perspectives that might enlighten the discussion of what the relationship might be between the individual and their participation in the IAP process. The three perspectives we examine are:

◊   Human development.

◊   Personality type.

◊   Group participation and individual choice.

### Human development

There is a substantial body of knowledge available in the area of human development. The study of how humans develop and become who they are, and attempts to explain how this process happens and how it can be influenced, has been the focus of psychology and its various fields.

The foundations of the study are found in the works of Freud and his contemporaries, including Adler and Jung. Adler focused on the challenge of individual development, referred to as 'individual psychology'. Adler was concerned about the relationship of the individual to the society in which he lives. The concept called '*gemeinscaftsgefuhl*' was coined to explore this relationship. Although it does not have a clear translation in English, the concept is best translated as 'social interest'. Adler saw this concept as:

> 'an innate counterforce, setting limits to the expansion tendency, aggression drive, lust for power.' (Manaster & Corsini, 1995, p.44).

Later Adlerians, such as Hertha Orgler, point out that:

> 'Adler does not want human herds, an objection often made; he does not want blind subordination, but open-eyed coordination. His ideal is not self-sacrifice, but self-development of the individual's abilities for his own good and for the good of humanity' (Manaster & Corsini, 1995, p.45).

Ansbacher said:

'... social interest actually means, not only an interest in others, but an interest in the interests of others.' (Manaster & Corsini, 1995, p.46)

And, the theory of individual psychology asserts:

'... that humans not only need other humans, but they also need to be needed, to have a feeling of belonging. Indeed, the absence of this feeling of belonging and of being wanted is probably the keenest and most devastating of all emotions, of being alone, being rejected, isolated.' (Manaster & Corsini, 1995, p.47)

These writers provide us with some understanding of the motivation towards participation. From an Adlerian perspective, the drive to self-development and the development of the other and the community are intertwined. It is not possible for the individual to develop effectively, without the development of interest in the welfare of others.

The concept of participation as a tool in self-development is also echoed in the thinking of Paulo Friere:

'Friere sees freedom as the "indispensable condition for the question for human completion"' (O'Connell, 1993)

On the theme of human development, Erickson (undated) has identified eight major psychosocial stages, which examine how we view ourselves and how we view ourselves in relation to others. These stages relate to our age profile but influence the adult behaviour in all of us. It is argued that the effectiveness of our management of each stage of the process influences our ability to deal with the next stage.

For those interested in facilitating the participation of others, this model represents a serious challenge to the capacity of professionals and others to bring about such participation. Where there has been a 'normal' process of development, the capacity of the individual to participate in any process will be enhanced. Where the development process has been interfered with in some way, the capacity of the individual to participate may be hampered and remedial action such as training, personal development, capacity-building and the use of creative and alternative participatory processes may need to be undertaken.

## Figure 5.3: Erickson's Psychosocial Stages

| Age | Major Psychosocial Crisis | |
|---|---|---|
| **First year** | Basic trust *vs.* Mistrust | Our experiences of the caretakers around us in our first year, and the level of love and attention we receive, determine whether we tend towards trust or mistrust. |
| **1 to 2** | Autonomy *vs.* Shame & doubt | This stage is where the child develops their own independence. They learn either to have courage and trust in their own abilities or to doubt that they are capable. |
| **3 to 5** | Initiative *vs.* Guilt | The stage of discovery, which if encouraged, gives us a sense of initiative and, if punished, results in suppressing our natural curiosity. |
| **6 to 12** | Industry *vs.* Inferiority | Those who receive 'encouragement' learn to develop a 'useful behaviour', whereas those who receive negative messages develop a sense of 'inferiority'. |
| **12 to 20** | Identity *vs.* Role Confusion | The individual develops a strong sense of self and their own values. This is a transition stage between the values of the parents and the adolescent's own values .When this stage does not develop well, the individual is left with a sense of role confusion and uncertainty. |
| **20 to 40** | Intimacy *vs.* Isolation | This is a critical stage for connection to others, where the individual chooses to make connections with others and to share intimately with others. |
| **40 to 65** | Generativity *vs.* Stagnation | Where the individual makes a contribution to the next generation. The alternative is the living-out of life without purpose. |
| **65+** | Integrity *vs.* Despair | The recognition of one's contribution to life. Successful management of this stage leads to wisdom or, alternatively, regret about all the things that might have been achieved. |

**Source:** Erickson (undated).

This linkage between the development of the individual and the connectedness with others has been taken up in recent years by Stephen Covey (1989). Covey's model explains the process of development as the move of the individual from dependence, through independence and the development of interdependence with others. Similar to the model suggested by Adler, Covey argues that the ultimate goal of human development is the ability of the individual to connect with others and to contribute to the welfare of others.

What Covey contributes to the thinking in this area is the notion of the factors/conditions that the individual needs to undertake in order to enable the individual to participate. He has identified two distinct phases in the process:

◊ **Stage 1:** The development from dependence to independence.

◊ **Stage 2:** The development from independence to interdependence.

Stage 1 of the process requires the individual to focus on their own internal processes. The challenge, Covey argues, is that human beings should:

◊ **Become pro-active rather than re-active:** Focus on what can be influenced and invest energy in making this happen. This is a mindset that does not look for someone else to blame when things go wrong but rather focuses on getting on to make the changes necessary.

◊ **Begin with the end in mind:** Having clear goals for oneself is essential to the development process. The alternative is that we drift and never succeed in achieving what we are capable of or indeed what we would wish for ourselves.

◊ **Put first things first:** Covey's model is grounded in the significance of ensuring that the actions of the individual should be in congruence with their values. Covey's model asserts that individuals need to be aware of what their priority values are and then ensure that their actions are in congruence with these values.

Stage 2 involves the development of attitudes that support this stage of development, such as:

◊ **Think win / win:** This is a particular frame of mind, which aims at ensuring that, in interactions with others, the objective of the interaction is to ensure that there is a positive outcome for both participants. In the context of theories of negotiation, this requires a different mindset to the one that aims to ensure that there is one winner. Fisher & Ury (1983), in their research, describe this as 'principled negotiation'.

◊ **Seek first to understand, and then to be understood:** This step suggests that, in communication with others, we need to aim to understand the perspective of the other, before we attempt to ensure that others understand us. This is a significant challenge, which requires the development of an 'other' focus. In practice, it requires the development of considerable listening skills. This type of listening requires that we attempt to reduce the impact of our own thoughts and attitudes when receiving information from others.

◊ **Synergise, using principles of creative co-operation:** This attitude is the most significant in the context of an IAP process. It relates to the ability of individuals to value difference, to build on strengths and to compensate for weaknesses, in order to create something that is greater than the sum of the individual parts.

◊ **Sharpen the saw:** The commitment of the individual over their own life-time to self-care and the development of their own potential.

The model could have significant implications for training in an IAP context. If, as Covey suggests, the ability of people to work together interdependently is governed by the development of the 'Seven Habits', and we accept that, in some cases at least, the seven-stage Erickson model does not work smoothly for everyone, then the adults who participate in the IAP process would benefit from significant training inputs. **Figure 5.4** suggests a template of possible training inputs that would be required.

### Figure 5.4: Training Opportunities, based on Covey's "Seven Habits"

| | Covey's 'Seven Habits' | Training Opportunity |
|---|---|---|
| 1 | **Be pro-active** | Self-awareness, assertiveness |
| 2 | **Begin with the end in mind** | Goal-setting for self and community |
| 3 | **Put first things first** | Exploring individual and collective values |
| 4 | **Think win / win** | Negotiation |
| 5 | **Seek first to understand and then to be understood** | Listening and communication |
| 6 | **Synergise** | Understanding of group process and interpersonal communication |
| 7 | **Sharpen the saw** | Refresher training and review sessions |

## Personality type and participation

The theories that explain personality type, and, in particular, the psychological types as used in the Myers Briggs-type Indicator (Briggs Myers *et al.*, 1998), are explored to determine what linkages there may be between these theories and the ability or motivation of individuals to participate.

There are many models that have examined personality type and, in many cases, these models are reflective of a particular psychological paradigm. Nonetheless, there have been some common themes that might be useful in the context of participation.

Most taxonomies of personality describe an 'Introversion/ Extroversion' dimension:

> '... an "introversion-extroversion" dimension, or a "moving away from people" *versus* a "moving toward people" orientation ... the general theory goes that individuals with relatively high internal levels of neural stimulation seek *quieter* surroundings (introverts), while those with relatively low internal levels of neural stimulation seek more *exciting* surroundings (extroverts), in order to maintain a comfortable internal equilibrium of neural stimulation.

> 'Since the mere presence of other people is physically arousing ... extroverts seek out others to raise their levels of arousal. Thus, for extroverts, through experience, the presence of others is rewarding. For introverts, the increased arousal levels may lead to feelings of shyness, or an increase in social anxiety. Thus, the presence of others may become associated with discomfort and a desire for solitude.' (Losh, 2005)

This, at least, suggests that there is a greater propensity for extroverts, rather than introverts, to participate in processes such as the IAP process. What the extroversion/introversion perspective also suggests is that the manner of participation between extroverts and introverts will be different. Briggs Myers *et al.* (1998) suggest, at a minimum, that extroverts will be more inclined to talk and, in so doing, will come to an understanding of the topic, while introverts will be more inclined to need thinking time before speaking. This simple hypothesis has implications for our expectations of who participates, but also influences our choice of the appropriate methodology for participation.

These are some of the implications for conducting IAP processes:

◊ It might lead us to hypothesise that extroverts will find public meetings and large group settings more comfortable than their introvert colleagues. Therefore, opportunities for individual conversation and consultation should be included in the process to facilitate the more introverted participants.

◊ In group settings, invitations to speak may encourage the introvert to participate.

◊ Time for reflection during discussion and debate might prove fruitful.

◊ Opportunities for written submission or feedback might be also be productive.

◊ Silence will be felt differently by the two groups, therefore, the extrovert will feel a two-second silence as being eternal, while, for an introvert, silences will be useful and helpful.

## Group participation and individual choice

Examining group theory for factors that influence the decision of an individual to participate the theory points to a number of interesting perspectives.

The first is obvious, and is reflective of the views presented by Erickson and Adler on the 'challenge' that is self-development. This maintains that the type of experience counts: people who have had generally supportive, positive experience with groups in the past will seek out others more often.

The 'exchange theory' suggests that, when the benefits of participating in the group are greater than the perceived costs, the choice will be to participate. Individuals receive benefits from groups, but also invest time, energy, money, and other resources in groups, thereby incurring costs. The significance of the costs and the benefits are determined by the individual, based on a variety of factors, including their personality type and life-cycle stage.

When joining a group, or participating in its activities, individuals may engage in a cost-benefit analysis, assessing the efforts they put into the group and the rewards they receive in return.

The model in **Figure 5.5** suggests that the individual's choice to participate is based on their calculation of the cost/benefit ratio. If the perceived benefits outweigh the cost, then the individual will participate, and will not, if the costs are greater.

The issue of similarity referred to above is particularly interesting. Similarity is probably the number one factor that turns up in research over and over, as individuals make decisions about participation. Similarity can be based on demographics and life-cycle variables (all young mothers), on values and attitudes, or on circumstances (Hurricane Katrina). Individuals see those who are similar to them and expect that the interaction will be 'comfortable'. A conversation with similar others is easy to initiate and continue; they have many more things in common; their behaviour appears more predictable and more familiar .The opportunity of interacting with those whom we perceive to be similar to us is seen as intrinsically rewarding:

> 'Festinger claimed that people avoid information that is likely to increase dissonance. Not only do we tend to select reading material and television programs that are consistent with our existing beliefs, we usually choose to be with people who are like us. By taking care to "stick with our own kind", we can maintain the relative comfort of the *status quo*. Like-minded people buffer us from ideas that could cause discomfort. In that sense, the process of making friends is an example of selecting our own propaganda.' (Griffin, 1997)

The perceived costs and benefits are likely to be calculated differently by individuals in different segments of the community, and socio-economic, educational, age and work factors will influence the decision-making process.

# Figure 5.5: The Cost/Benefit of Participation

| Rewards | Costs | Implications for the IAP Process |
|---|---|---|
| **Access to group resources, including status and prestige** | **Time** | If the individual believes that they can have access to resources that they value, then the choice will be to invest their time in the process. This brings up interesting questions around the nature of the resources available to the group in an IAP process and the values that the individual might give to such resources. |
| **Other goal attainments, impossible to achieve alone** | **Effort** | If the individual believes that, only through the participation of others, will a goal that is significant to them be achieved, then the choice will be made to participate. The interesting questions that this gives rise to are what the goals of the individuals might be and issues about the ability of the individual to work with others. |
| **Socio-emotional benefits, gained from interaction with attractive others** | **Energy** | The concept of attractiveness is an interesting one. What makes others attractive to us? The theory suggests that we are attracted to people who are similar to ourselves: similar in socio/economic/personality profile to us. This concept of attractiveness is discussed further below. This presents a particular challenge to the IAP process in including those individuals who may be more marginalized in the community. The ability of a group to be sufficiently adaptable to be 'attractive' to all individuals in the community is problematic. |
| **Alleviation of loneliness** | **Financial investments** | The need for 'belonging' is a recognised and accepted human need. The individual who perceives that there is an opportunity to relieve their loneliness by joining in a group process is likely to do so. The cost of this membership is in the financial cost of joining or having to invest in the actions of the group. In an IAP context, this suggests that the process may be attractive to people who are lonely and that costs such as childcare and even that of driving to meetings might be a disincentive to others to join or participate in groups. |
| **A sense of belonging and contribution to one's social or collective identity** | **Confrontational situations with others, especially when disagreements occur over goals or courses of action** | The factors identified above are continued in this heading. In addition to belonging to a group and the alleviation of loneliness, the group itself and membership of the group can contribute to the individual's sense of self. The challenge for the IAP process is that, if the group is perceived to consist of some type of 'in' group, it may prove unattractive to others. In the course of the process, disagreement is likely to occur and the challenge is to provide mechanisms to enable individuals to manage this confrontation purposefully. |

Life-cycle theory suggests that where people are on the life-cycle influences their decision to participate – for example, parents with young children are less likely to participate in the IAP process, because the perceived costs (away from children in evening, cost of childminding, time pressure, etc.) are greater than the perceived benefits that might come from participating. This tends to have a greater impact on women than on men, and is reflected in the patterns of participation that have been observed in the IAP process.

Additional factors that influence the decision of individuals to joining groups include factors such as:

◊ **Propinquity:** The group is convenient, nearby. Very often, we interact with the same people who are close by on a continuous basis. We know from the 'mere exposure' literature that, other things equal, the more we are exposed to something and the more familiar it is, the more we like that person or entity.

◊ **Recruitment:** Group members want the individual to join. Often this is because people the individual already knows are members.

## PARTICIPATION IN PRACTICE – THE IAP EXPERIENCE

Elsewhere in this book, the processes and mechanisms of the IAP process are discussed. In the IAP process, the participation mechanisms that have been used are:

◊ Steering group meetings.

◊ Focus group meetings.

◊ Written surveys.

◊ Interviews.

In the context of the IAP process, the aim is to include the views of all the relevant stakeholders and to facilitate a process whereby these views are assimilated, to create a plan for the community for a period of years into the future. Therefore, this requires the following:

◊  That individuals from each of the stakeholding groups
   participate in the process.

◊  That the nature of that participation is such as to ensure that a
   process is in place that allows these (sometimes opposite) views
   to be articulated and then to be assimilated into a coherent plan.

◊  That, at the completion of the plan, the participants are
   committed to the plan, so as to ensure its implementation.

To this end, the following data emerged from the experience of the IAP
process in one area.

The IAP process concept requires participation from all levels in the
community and all sectors in the community. A stratified approach
suggests the following categorisations for inclusion:

| **Categorisations:** |
| --- |
| **Age:** <25, 25-50, >50 |
| **Economic:** Unemployed, employed, self-employed, retired |
| **Gender**: Male/Female |

Studies of one group that participated in the IAP process show the total
population of this community was 532 and the numbers who
participated at any stage of the process represent 10% of the total
population. The pattern of participation is also interesting and the
**Figure 5.6** shows a pattern of participation, which shows that, of the 52
people who participated at any stage in the project, less than 50%
attended 50% of the meetings.

The figures for participation based on age profile (**Figure 5.7**) are not
very promising, showing that the participation of people less than 25
years of age was non-existent. This gives rise to concern, in the context
of the development of a model for a community for the future. The
participants were equally divided between those who were between 25
and 50 years of age and those who were over the age of 50. This is
reflective of the life-cycle model, discussed earlier, where those who
have time to participate are more likely to be of mature years.

In other areas of IAP development, schools have been approached
and, where youth organisations are available, these can be mobilised to
participate. For younger people, it is important that the use of creative

techniques, especially visual tools, be included, to enable the younger people to participate in these processes.

## Figure 5.6: The Pattern of Participation

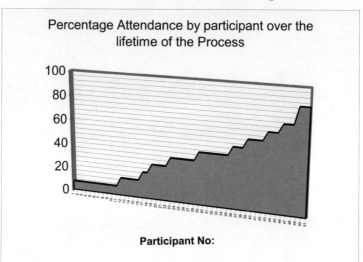

## Figure 5.7: The Age Profile of Participants

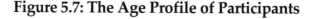
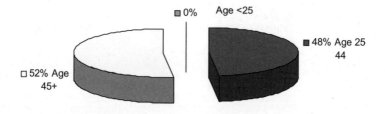

The use of the meeting as the core method of measuring the extent of the participation has influenced these results. The use of focus groups, questionnaires, task groups and informal interactions were not analysed in these figures. It is reasonable to assume that such analysis would increase the 'rate' of participation, but perhaps would also have influenced the 'depth' of participation by each individual. It is important to point out also that the data collected during these additional processes was reflected in the IAP document produced. What emerges is a need to conduct research into both of these issues and to include in the analysis the use of alternative participatory methods.

## Figure 5.8: Participation Pattern by Gender at Steering Group Meetings

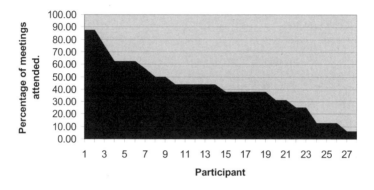

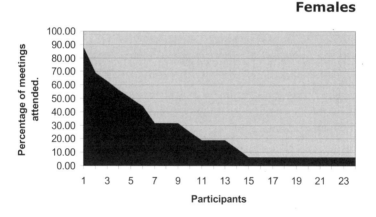

**Figure 5.8** demonstrates that there is a lower pattern of attendance by women over the lifetime of the process and that, as the period of the project extended, the decline in female participation was more significant than that of the male cohort. It would be interesting to explore why this might be the case.

## RECOMMENDATIONS

◊ There is a need to gather more data on participation levels in the IAP process. It would be useful to gather more quantitative data at each stage of the process and qualitative data at significant points in the process.

◊ There is a need to be aware of the limitations that exist on the ability of individuals to participate in group processes and, as a consequence, to make use of alternative participatory methods to ensure that participation.

◊ There is also a need to explore expectations around expected participation levels with the steering group at an early stage in the process. There is a need to provide appropriate training to participants in such processes, at all the levels suggested in the Covey model above.

## CONCLUSIONS

The paper has explored the issue of participation in the IAP process by looking at the experience from the perspective of the individual. To this end, it has explored some of the theory in relation to human development, personality theory and group work that provide a perspective that can help to inform our understanding of the individual choice to participate and the nature of that participation. A preliminary look at information gathered from the TI experience of participation in the IAP process provides some interesting data in this regard. What emerges is a need to use this understanding to inform the training/coaching element of the IAP process, to develop a range of techniques that enhance the participation of the individual and to conduct further research that will provide information to enable us to understand this complex issue better in an Irish context.

# 6

# GIS APPLICATIONS IN IAP

## *Martin McCormack*

Planning substantially presumes upon accurate information being readily available. It is a forward-looking process that draws upon various types of data, and analysis of such information, to produce outcomes consistent with an overall philosophy. Insofar as community-based planning is concerned, the interaction of planning methodologies, consultation processes, feasibility studies and physical parameters, as well as policy frameworks, all lead to the gradual development of 'a plan'. When undertaking an Integrated Area Planning (IAP) process, the plan is but one of the outcomes of an overall process that draws on theories and practices associated with community development, land-use management, economic planning, environmental management, infrastructure development, cultural heritage and social services provision. As with many other types of planning, IAPs require a significant amount of information/data, both to inform the process itself and also to help develop future strategies and programmes.

Increasingly, planners, and others involved in land-use management who are concerned about the impact that certain types of development may have on the environment, are undertaking modelling exercises to help determine any such impacts. Undoubtedly, therefore, the quality and analysis of data has a significant bearing on the outcomes from any planning process.

Geographic information systems (GIS) have been developed to help provide information in a spatial context. Visual representation of data benefits all who are involved in an IAP process, but has a special benefit for those who may find it easier to relate to spatially-presented data rather than to a written report or plan. It helps community members and others engaged in the process to identify readily with existing and proposed considerations, particularly in areas having some physical outcomes or parameters. Therefore, it facilitates a greater level of engagement in the overall process than might otherwise be the case, and leads to a more comprehensive development and selection of best available options. The participation of community members in mapping exercises (such as the identification of local sites/features of importance, mapping of existing and proposed road and footpath options, etc.) can lead to a plan that has been 'proofed' to a higher degree than would otherwise be possible. The development of skills in relation to map-reading and map preparations has potential benefits from a capacity-building perspective also.

## ADVANTAGES OF GIS IN IAP

GIS in the IAP process:

◊ Facilitates greater participation in community development.

◊ Facilitates greater interaction between local authorities, communities and other stakeholders.

◊ Helps in providing a better understanding of the context within which planning decisions are made (social, economic, cultural, geographical).

◊ Helps communities to develop, articulate and present views on issues of concern.

◊ Helps to ensure that outcomes are consistent with stated objectives.

◊ Allows settlement patterns to be explored and future needs to be met.

◊ Helps to ensure best environmental management practice, as visual components (maps) provide a readily-understandable and identifiable framework for all (including those who may find difficulties relating to written reports).

◊ Allows for the development of options related to development planning, and facilitates the adoption of best practicable solutions.

◊ Facilitates monitoring, and evaluation and outputs can be updated readily as time progresses.

◊   Helps to identify readily issues of concern (derelict buildings, pollution, location of services, etc.).

Essentially, GIS helps us to look at information somewhat differently than might otherwise be the case. The spatial context itself can be land-based, water-based, air-based, etc. and the outcome from a typical GIS exercise is a presentation of information on a map that can be examined. The information collected, and which forms the basis of the map itself (such as population distributions, river water quality, etc.), usually requires the development of a link between a database containing population statistics, for instance, and a digital map. GIS can play a major role in an IAP process, as it allows for the use of information gathered at local level and also information that can be based on a sophisticated level of data collection (such as air quality data). Information presented in a graphical format can lead ultimately to a better understanding of the context and environment within which the planning exercise is taking place, and also to more realistic outcomes based on any proposed planning processes. Being able to examine and to represent information in ways that allow different combinations of variables to be combined, leads ultimately to more informed decision-making processes. An important key feature of a typical GIS system is an ability to layer information (such as a map of proposed roads, which can be placed upon an existing physical map, showing all physical features).

## INFORMATION REQUIREMENTS FOR AN IAP

The information requirements for a planning process, such as an IAP process, typically include:

◊   Local population characteristics.

◊   Local geographical and physical characteristics.

◊   Environmental resources and quality of environment.

◊   Economic resources.

◊   Infrastructure resources.

◊   Cultural/historical characteristics.

◊   Social services provision.

## Local population

A typical IAP is often based in a rural area that has a village/town element. The actual plan boundaries may be parish-based, townland-based or based on defined electoral areas, such as District Electoral Divisions (DEDs). Where local population statistics are concerned, Central Statistics Office data is normally used. This data, which typically is based on DEDs, can also be obtained for smaller areas (small area population statistics – SAPS). This data can provide information on:

◊ General demographic trends.

◊ Socio-economic indicators (household composition, employment/unemployment, etc.).

◊ Access to services (transport).

Of particular use from a planning context is the representation of trends (such as population decline associated with certain areas, key employment/unemployment characteristics, household composition, etc.). With a continuing decline in the average size of households in Ireland, for instance, the country has witnessed a significant increase in the number of housing units being constructed. Many smaller towns and villages have witnessed changes to the overall shape of the town/village and such shapes have had not insignificant landscape impacts.

## Geography

The geographical characteristics of an area are unique and, typically, are represented on maps, varying in scale from 1:1000 to 1:50,000, depending on the size of area. A good knowledge and appreciation of the geographical characteristics (shape, landscape features, topography, etc.) helps to assign particular designations to different elements of the area, which, in turn, better inform the decision-making process. Land-based characteristics influence population profiles. In Ireland, population densities in many areas are closely related to physical features, such as road networks, water bodies, boglands, mountains and valleys. Much of the settlement patterns of today are based on physical constraints and opportunities that shaped the establishment of towns and cities in the past. Typically, along coastal areas, these included the potential for port facilities, while, in inland areas, the availability of good agricultural land helped to establish centres of settlement, such as market towns. In more recent times, and with the changes in employment patterns (significant decrease in those involved in full-time farming and a significant increase in those employed in the services sector), Ireland has witnessed, particularly since the mid 1990s, notable increases in populations of the larger urban conurbations. This is particularly true for urban centres within 'commuting distance' of the main cities, but also for villages that, until recently, would have struggled even to maintain their small population numbers.

## Figure 6.1: Map showing percentage population change (1996 – 2006) for Co. Offaly by DED

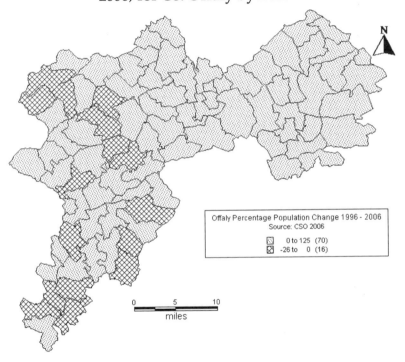

**Source:** *Ordnance Survey Ireland Permit No. 8217; © Ordnance Survey Ireland/Government of Ireland*

For those settlements with adequate services (sewage and water), population growth has sometimes been of the order of over 60% (Kinnegad in Co. Westmeath recorded an increase of 150% between 1996 and 2002 (CSO, 2002)), while, in many other rural settlements without adequate services, the change has been much smaller, and sometimes even negative.

**Figure 6.2: Shannonbridge DED & Surrounding DEDs (in Offaly, Roscommon & Galway)**

Source: *Ordnance Survey Ireland Permit No. 8217;* © *Ordnance Survey Ireland/Government of Ireland*

## Figure 6.3: Shannonbridge & Surrounding DEDs – Number of houses built per DED (1996-2006)

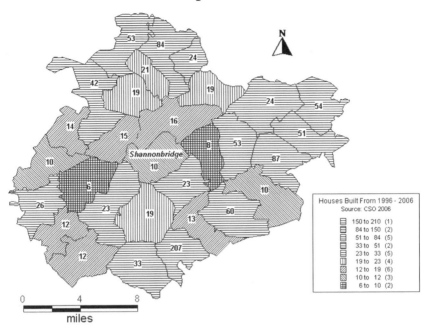

Source: *Ordnance Survey Ireland Permit No. 8217;* © *Ordnance Survey Ireland/Government of Ireland*

## Environmental resources

Environmental resources (including the built and natural environment) help provide historical perspectives, contemporary viewpoints and future visions for areas undergoing a planning process. The location of villages and towns, the distribution of residential units, village structures, etc. are often based on environmental characteristics (location of water supplies/river crossings/availability of raw materials/harbour facilities). With the increased range of diverse economic activities, the links between origin of place and planning perspectives is assumed and successive layers of development can either compound or enhance such assumptions.

With the development of more comprehensive environmental management strategies, plans can now be screened for a range of environmental issues, including traffic management, ground water protection, waste arisings, etc. GIS is an essential tool in planning for environmental sustainability and helps to ensure that existing resources are adequately managed and that negative impacts can be avoided or mitigated against.

The development of watershed models for the overall management of water bodies in Ireland and elsewhere has brought a more regional focus to county and local planning processes. Similarly, the designation of certain areas, such as Special Areas of Conservation, brings a broader perspective to the management of environmental resources.

## Figure 6.4:  Nature Designations at Kinvara, Co. Galway

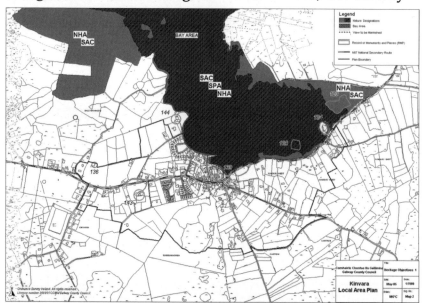

Source: *Ordnance Survey Ireland Permit No. 8217; © Ordnance Survey Ireland/Government of Ireland; © Galway County Council*

GIS enables such broader perspectives to be appraised by communities, and to be incorporated into local development plans. Just as it is important for those operating in a planning context at county, regional and national levels to have an understanding of community and local development issues, so too it is important for communities to have an understanding of the wider environmental and socio-economic context within which development processes occur. The management of environmental resources calls for effective policies and structures at all appropriate levels. Local ownership of environmental issues can be facilitated best through an increased understanding of, and participation in, processes aimed at helping to ensure environmental sustainability. The IAP process facilitates such participation by all stakeholders in the development of programmes at local level aimed at establishing and operating best practice in environmental management at local level.

## Economic and infrastructural resources

The changes that have occurred in the landscape of Ireland in recent years, particularly in urban areas, have been driven largely by economic factors. As Ireland's economy has developed, population growth has been witnessed in many areas, a situation that is in sharp contrast to decades of decline. The need to provide adequately for continued economic development, through the provision of enterprise areas, serviced sites, etc. can only be done in the context of good forward planning strategies, coupled with investment in infrastructure development. A constraint, commonly encountered throughout Ireland regarding economic and residential development, is that of lack of adequate waste-water treatment capacity. While some major investments have taken place in the larger urban centres, many towns and villages with populations of less than 2,000 persons, are still awaiting investment in treatment plants and associated infrastructure. In response to the need for more balanced regional development, the Government published the *National Spatial Strategy* in 2002. This strategy proposed an interlocking framework of gateways and hubs throughout the country. This overall strategy sets a new context for planning in rural areas, and establishes an overall view of future national development. Where smaller population centres are concerned, however, there is no similar framework in place, which, in turn, points to the need for coherent strategies for such areas, including small towns and villages.

GIS applications can allow for a systematic approach to economic development, through the representation of best options for enterprise and commercial developments. In the case of Ferbane in Co. Offaly, economic development was a key target of the community, and was seen as a potential means of redressing population decline and of counteracting the recent loss of employment opportunities caused by the decommissioning of a local power station.

**Figure 6.5: Draft Proposals for Land-use at Ferbane,
Co. Offaly (c.2001)**

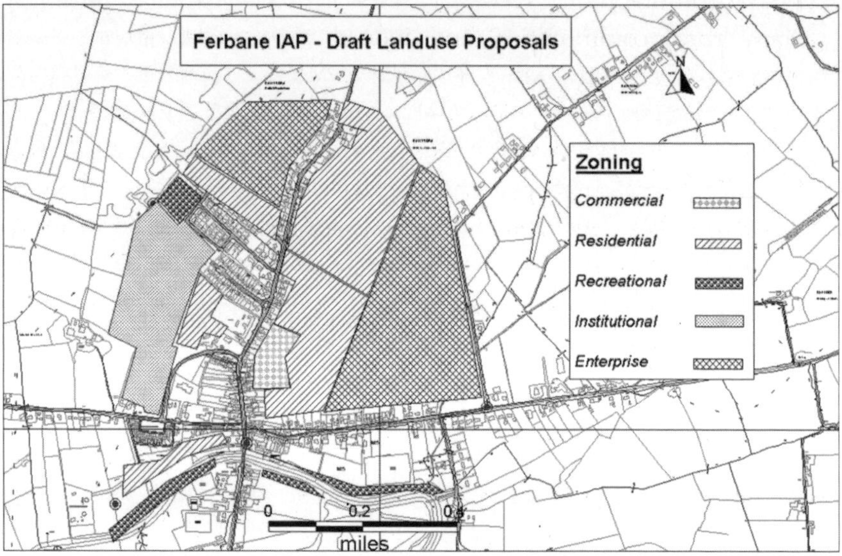

Source: *Ordnance Survey Ireland Permit No. 8217; © Ordnance
Survey Ireland/Government of Ireland*

The community, working in co-operation with Offaly Co. Council and facilitated by TI, produced a series of options relating to overall future development within the town. On the basis of this exercise, and of further work by the Ferbane Development Group, an enterprise area has been developed that has seen the provision of enterprise units within the area. The applicability of GIS in providing accurate representations of various options for development within the town and its environs led to the approval by the local authority of a community-driven local enterprise development. This also followed on from the data collection exercise, which revealed that a number of local businesses would expand their businesses and that lack of available space to do so was a constraint.

In Eyrecourt in east Galway, a survey undertaken by the community revealed that there had been a substantial loss of businesses over the years, with many traditional businesses having become unsustainable. These ranged from drapery shops to butcher shops and, while the village had relatively good infrastructure in terms of buildings, a decline in population and changes in agricultural policies, as well as improved transport availability at household level, meant that businesses could not operate profitably.

Many rural communities, and indeed towns with strong rural hinterlands, are experiencing changing economic fortunes, due to a variety of factors. Some of these factors (mobile workforce and employment opportunities, reduced number of people working in full time farming, changes in primary and secondary production patterns, increased services sector, etc.) have had positive economic benefits, while others have not. This latter scenario is more pronounced in areas that have had only one or two main employers/employment types. In some instances, such scenarios can lead to a 'cycle of deprivation'. Policies aimed at addressing such challenges can be facilitated at local level through integrated planning programmes, which have the ability to identify the interlocking mechanisms that contribute to economic disadvantage and which can also facilitate an appropriate set of responses at local level.

### Figure 6.6: Map Showing Derelict Buildings in Eyrecourt, Co. Galway (based on 2004 survey)

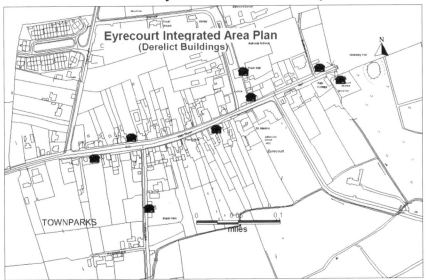

Source: Ordnance Survey Ireland Permit No. 8217; © Ordnance Survey Ireland/Government of Ireland

## Culture and history

The cultural trademarks of different areas are of critical importance in maintaining identity. An understanding of culture, and cultural associations with music, food, sport or indeed the built or natural environment, is essential in any sustainable planning context. Conversely, a lack of understanding of local culture and traditions by planners and others engaged in planning processes can often serve to disengage and to alienate communities from such processes. Some of the most recent controversies in Ireland in relation to cultural issues have been associated with major road infrastructure works at Tara in Co. Meath and at Carrickmines in Co. Dublin. While these are related to large scale projects, for most small towns and villages, the issues of cultural identity may relate to historic sites, such as castles or demesne houses, or even to traditions, including pilgrimages, food preparations, etc.

GIS has been used to ensure that associations with traditions can be preserved and enhanced, and that cultural issues are adequately reflected in planning processes. The degree to which an IAP process allows for the exploration of issues, ranging from cultural identity to environmental protection, can be significant, given the particular circumstances in which the plan is being developed.

## Social services provision

The access to, and provision of, social services (whether in relation to health care or transport services) are essential determinants in the quality of life of people living in rural areas and in small settlements. Indeed, the term 'rural' often denotes a 'sense of place', rather than a defined entity. Just as there are 'contested countryside cultures', so there are contested views of 'the rural'. In any event, the IAP process often takes place in areas of population of less than 1,500 persons (small towns/villages) and, as such, it is common for these areas to lack many of the services associated with larger settlements. By helping to identify the resources that are available within the plan's catchment area, the process can help focus resources in a spatial context. For example, public transport in Ireland has been dominated mostly by inter-city transport networks that often bypass rural communities, especially those not located along main routes. This is in sharp contrast to urban transport networks, which often have a multitude of services available within the functional urban boundaries. GIS applications also can be used to help determine the effective catchment areas of schools, health centres and even commercial elements, such as retail outlets. With increased pressure for places a common feature of many schools in rural areas that are located in close proximity to main towns, the necessary development of school infrastructure is frequently much later than that of housing developments.. GIS can help model for, and correlate, increases in population within defined boundaries with social services provision, so that improved delivery of services can occur.

## PLANNING FOR SUSTAINABILITY: OPTIMISING RESOURCES & PREPARING FOR CHANGE

The IAP process helps with the identification of key local priorities. Often, for these priorities to be addressed, certain related issues need also to be dealt with. For example, when a community decides that it would like to see its population increase by 50% over a period of five years or thereabouts, planners need to ensure that there is sufficient land zoned to cater for this and associated needs. These related issues or conditionalities can be addressed best in a participative fashion, where all relevant stakeholders can agree on the outcomes. Ultimately, local councillors agree on such issues and vote on proposals for change of use of such areas. Proposed outcomes are based on conditionalities being achieved, and the process allows for actions to be implemented based on this framework. These conditionalities can be achieved through the development of options based on sustainability criteria and GIS allows such criteria to be readily identified.

In the case of Kinvara, the community agreed broad parameters, such as the scale and pace of development, a limit on certain types of development until adequate waste water facilities were in place, the preservation of certain views and green areas, etc. The development of a Local Area Plan by Galway Co. Council, which was substantially based on the IAP, allowed for further public consultation on these and other related issues.

The concept of sustainability is not new and elements of sustainable development have been incorporated into planning policies for some time. In more recent times, the development of frameworks associated with the concept has progressed and these, in turn, have been reflected in the Planning & Development Act 2000 and in the associated Regulations of 2001. One of the realities that such frameworks show is that there needs to be an integration of many of the agreed philosophies that form part of the framework. While this may seem easy to conceptualise, it is not always easy to work out in practice, and it calls for a significant amount of time being given over to policy formulation. In the case of integrated area planning, the formulation of such policies forms a large part of the development of the resultant plan. The further integration of the IAP into the LAP and any County Development Plan calls for coherent policy formulation at community and at county levels. Again, this is not always easy to secure and calls for a commitment from local authorities to support actively and to guide development processes at local level.

In relation to land-use planning, one increasingly important factor is the optimum use of land through increased residential densities. In turn, this needs to be balanced by having an increase in recreational and amenity space availability, so that the overall quality of life of communities is not compromised. Likewise, the development of adequate waste treatment facilities has meant that many elements of such plans may remain aspirational at best, unless matched with funding commitments from local authorities, as well as from central government.

From an environmental management perspective, the lack of adequate infrastructure has meant that waste management has not kept pace with development and has been a constraint to development in many areas. While there have been substantial improvements in general in the performance of many key environmental indicators in Ireland in recent years (such as a decline in the number of 'seriously polluted' water bodies), the development of initiatives (such as Local Agenda 21) has not been reflected to any major degree in planning at local level. This is not to say that planning for local areas has not taken place, but that full engagement has not occurred as well as it might have done. One means of addressing this, in the context of integrated area planning, is to use concepts such as 'green maps', which enable communities to participate in the development of locally-produced maps that reflect the main environmental features of their areas. These maps can also be used to help establish and to monitor indicators and objectives. While the concept has been applied at locations as diverse as New York city and

Victoria Falls, it has not been widely used in local area planning. Nonetheless, it has obvious benefits from a community and sustainable planning perspective.

### Figure 6.7: Community Proposals for Improved Paths & Lighting for Hacketstown, Co. Carlow

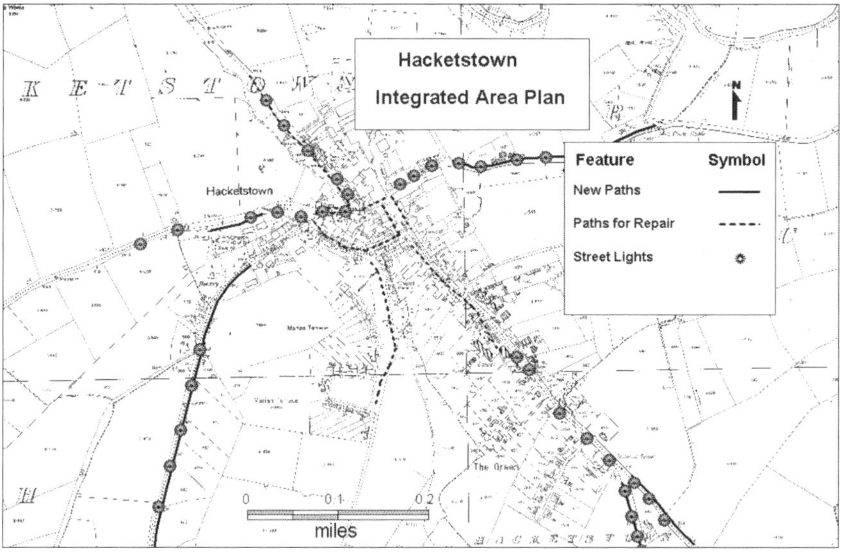

Source: *Ordnance Survey Ireland Permit No. 8217; © Ordnance Survey Ireland/Government of Ireland*

The creation of a sense of ownership around environmental resources is essential, if such resources are to be managed in a fashion that will benefit present and future generations. The involvement of all sectors of a community, including school children and the elderly, is necessary, if there is to be a sharing of knowledge and skills around the environment, so that the concept becomes more meaningful. This can be facilitated readily through GIS, which accommodates the concept of 'layering', whereby different elements can be incorporated onto one map. It can be used to help determine certain landscape and visual impacts of proposals, through the determination and representation of zones of visual influence, which are related to the scale of proposed developments, as well as to existing landscape features.

Community involvement in other elements of planning, such as traffic management and road safety, has obvious benefits also. Planning for sustainability implies being pro-active, rather than merely being reactive. Insofar as most planning in Ireland is carried out currently, a community often only gets their first opportunity to become involved in decision-making processes once maps (often with various options indicated) have been developed. This can lead to communities feeling marginalised through the process and to the establishment of adversarial positions among many stakeholders. IAP allows for the development of these options through the process rather than at the initial stages of consultation, and the development of policy objectives by the community can provide more readily an accepted rationale for the proposals, as mapped. Thus, even the development of the options themselves becomes a significant part of the process.

The participation by community members in decision-making processes is a prerequisite for effective planning and good local government. During the IAP process, the establishment within communities of structures such as steering groups and task groups helps to ensure that there is a coherent community-based framework, capable of representing the overall community in matters affecting community life.

## CONCLUSION

IAP represents a more comprehensive planning methodology to deal with issues affecting the lives of rural communities. It is a participative process and, by its nature, calls for a greater degree of effort from all stakeholders than might otherwise be the case. It also offers a greater degree of flexibility in dealing with issues that are of local concern, whether these be economic, social, cultural or environmental. Unlike statutory plans for local areas (Local Area Plans), it can deal with issues not only within defined settlement areas but also in the wider areas, often parish-based. This, in turn, helps to provide a more true reflection of the dynamics of rural areas and, consequently, improved decision-making at community level is possible. The involvement of farmers, for example, as a specific category under the process helps to ensure that there is an appropriate rural focus and that more balanced objectives are developed.

Being founded on a pro-active philosophy, the process aims to present information and to represent issues as comprehensively as possible. Planning itself is an ongoing process and it is important to reflect the changing patterns around us. The use of GIS in the IAP process helps to reflect this.

The advantages of using GIS in community-based planning exercises such as IAPs can be summarised as follows:

◊ It facilitates greater participation in community development, as well as providing a focus for harnessing community energy.

◊ It helps to identify and to assess the spatial context of development indicators, commonly achieved through the use of CSO data, although data collected at household level can also be used.

◊ It facilitates greater interaction between local authorities, communities and other stakeholders in the process. GIS provides a means whereby the expertise of local authorities can be used in representing community objectives. Communities are often assisted with maps and other elements of development plans to help them represent better their environment and to plan for its future development.

◊ It helps to ensure that outcomes are consistent and that objectives are reflected in future planning decisions. It allows a proofing of some objectives and allows communities to correlate proposals in relation to future population growth with areas proposed for zoning.

◊ It allows settlement patterns to be explored and future needs to be met. This facilitates better planning through an improved understanding of population trends, unemployment trends, educational attainment, etc.

◊ It helps ensure best environmental management practice. The management of the environmental is seen as a more comprehensive framework of policies, programmes and actions than was previously the case. The greater involvement of communities in environmental management (and a greater awareness at local level of community issues) is essential for best practice to be established. This is facilitated through the development and mapping of local environmental objectives, whether these include the preservation of certain features or views or the mapping of indicators of pollution.

◊ Having a visual component (namely maps), it provides a readily understandable and identifiable framework for all (including those who may find difficulties relating to written reports). Individuals tend to absorb more from an image than through the exhaustive reading of reports. The visual presentation of information is important, as it serves to illustrate/represent a physical or other entity. It also has an importance apart from the representation of the element(s) being mapped, namely that it helps people engage with the elements being mapped in a manner that would not otherwise be possible, as it allows individuals and the community as a whole to reflect upon the spatial nature and context of those elements.

◊ It allows for the development of options related to development planning and facilitates the adoption of best practicable options. This is often seen when land-use issues arise and the community develops, appraises and selects options appropriate to their areas.

◊ Outputs can be altered and upgraded as time progresses. Monitoring and evaluation are essential to the development of any planning process. GIS facilitates such monitoring and evaluation, as data is stored digitally so that it can be accessed and manipulated readily.

◊ It helps to readily identify issues of concern (derelict buildings, pollution, location of services, etc.). The simple depiction of features, such as derelict buildings in a streetscape, helps to identify and to prioritise issues for action.

# 7

# MAKING LOCAL DEVELOPMENT PLANS: THE IRISH EXPERIENCE

## *Ciaran Lynch*

Though little research has been done on the matter, it is clear from anecdotal evidence, the comments of elected members and ongoing media discussion, that land-use planning in the Republic of Ireland is a highly conflicted activity. It is one of the principal items of attention in the local and regional media, as well as from time to time in the national media, and many locally-elected councillors state that it is the single activity that absorbs the greatest amount of their time.

Land-use planning conflicts, of course, are inevitable, given the range of opinions on how land should be managed and the unequal distribution of the costs and benefits that arise. However, the nature and structure of local government in Ireland, as well as the various implied and actual wrong-doing that has taken place within the planning system, have bestowed a more adversarial quality than necessary on the policy-making processes that surround land-use and environmental management. The process has set official against councillor, community against official and, indeed, official against official, on a far more regular basis than is healthy.

There are, no doubt, many reasons for the emergence of this situation. However, the model of policy-making that is used in Ireland with regard to land-use planning has tended to be prescriptive and expert-led, while lodged within a structure that emphasises participation and democratic control. This dislocation between practice and structure may have contributed to the conflicted and adversarial model of planning that we now experience, and the time has come to consider whether other models could serve us better.

An OECD report, *Citizens as Partners: Information, Consultation & Public Participation in Policy-Making*, (OECD, 2001) identified three areas, under which citizen participation in policy-making can be analysed:

◊ The legislative context.

◊ The policy context.

◊ The institutional context.

This provides a useful model that can be applied to the system of land-use development plan making in the Republic of Ireland. Firstly, however, it is important to consider the nature of the Irish system of local government, in terms of the role given to it to represent the interests of local citizens.

## THE LOCAL GOVERNMENT SYSTEM

Local government in the Republic of Ireland has now been recognised, both in the Constitution and in the Local Government Act 2001, as a basic element of Irish democracy. For example, Article 28a of the Constitution states that:

'The State recognises the role of local government in providing a forum for the democratic representation of local communities, in exercising and performing at local level powers and functions conferred by law and in promoting by its initiatives the interests of such communities.'

This article, which was adopted by a referendum in 1999, is a clear indication of the role of local government and is further developed in legislation. For example, section 63 of the Local Government Act 2001 states that:

'The functions of a local authority are:

(*a*) to provide a forum for the democratic representation of the local community, in accordance with section 64, and to provide civic leadership for that community, (*b*) to carry out such functions as may at any material time stand conferred on the relevant authority by or under any enactment (including this Act and any other enactment whether enacted before or after this Act),

(*c*) to carry out any ancillary functions under section 65, and

(*d*) to take such action as it considers necessary or desirable to promote the community interest in accordance with section 66.

Section 64 expands on the statement of the local authority's representative role, stating that:

'... as a forum for the democratic representation of the local community, a local authority may represent the interests of such community in such manner as it thinks appropriate.'

It also outlines some of the specific things that a local authority may do with respect to this aspect of its role:

'... a local authority may:

(*a*) ascertain and communicate to other local authorities and public authorities the views of the local community in relation to matters as respects which those other authorities perform functions and which affect the interests of the administrative area of the authority and the local community,

(*b*) promote, organise or assist the carrying out of research, surveys (including public opinion surveys) or studies with respect to the local community or its administrative area,

(*c*) facilitate and promote interest and involvement in local government affairs generally,

(*d*) promote interest among young people in democracy and local government and in community and civic affairs generally.'

This element of the legislation indicates clearly the intention of the legislature that local authorities would be clear as to the interests of the communities that they represent and that they would have regard to these needs when coming to decisions on how, and on what matters, to pursue their representative role.

The land-use planning system is an element of local government that has specific processes assigned to it regarding these matters. The issue is whether these processes are used in a way that reflects the intention of the local government legislation.

## LAND–USE PLANNING

Land-use planning in the Republic of Ireland is one of the most decentralised aspects of government in the country. Within guidelines set by national government and regional authorities, it is left largely to local planning authorities to decide on the policies that they should adopt for their areas and to make decisions on specific planning applications that are the basis for the implementation of the adopted policies.

The Irish planning system is governed by the Planning & Development Act 2000 and the Regulations made under it. The system is very much based on the UK model, in that it is a 'policy and licence' rather than a 'zoning ordinance'-based approach.

The policy elements of the system are contained in the development plans that are made by each planning authority, while the licensing system consists primarily of a process through which formal application is made for permission to carry out development, which cannot be commenced until permission is granted. The system is completed by a set of enforcement procedures that can be used against those who do not seek permission or who carry out development in ways that are not in accordance with approved plans.

Applications for permission are made to the relevant planning authority and the authority's decision can be appealed to An Bórd Pleanála, an independent planning appeals board. Like all administrative bodies, the planning authorities are also open to court action on the grounds of failure of due process.

In theory, the Irish planning system facilitates higher levels of participation than the UK system. For example, any person, whether affected or not, is entitled to comment on proposed plans and policies, to raise objections to specific development proposals and to appeal the decisions of the local authority to An Bórd Pleanála.

However, despite the theoretical openness of the system, public participation has been far greater with regard to planning applications than it has been with regard to the planning policy development system:

'… many local authorities in Ireland receive a relatively poor response when they invite comments on their draft five-year development plan for the area, or hold public meetings on the subject. However, when an application for a large development project is lodged, hundreds or sometimes thousands of observations can be received.' (Callanan, 2003, p.3)

The situation does not seem to be any better in the UK. Writing in the *Planning Inspectorate Journal*, Silvera noted that:

'Despite the efforts of central and local government awareness and participation, particularly among disadvantaged communities, remains low and many people do not come into contact with the planning system unless their amenities or interests are directly affected by a development proposal. Even where local communities are pro-active, they are often faced with a large volume of legislation, complex procedures, jargon and a wealth of government guidance and policy.' (Silvera, 2000)

It is also interesting to note that, while the UK Government's statement of its e-planning vision includes a reference to participation in policy-making, the actual service provision it discusses for public and community stakeholders relates almost exclusively to services for development control customers. Compare its statement of vision:

'A world class e-planning service will deliver new, more efficient ways of *enabling the community to engage in developing a shared vision for their local area* [italics added], easier access to high-quality, relevant, information and guidance and, streamlined processes for sharing and exchanging information amongst key players.' (Department for Communities & Local Government (UK), 2007))

with the following:

'The typical interactions of the public with the planning system will be one-off transactions, non-expert users, mostly local focus, mostly free, a wide variety of access channels, a self-service and consumer focus.' (Department for Communities & Local Government (UK), 2007)

It may be suggested, of course, that it is easier to engage with the issues surrounding specific concrete proposals than it is to participate in discussions on complex and multi-faceted policy. However, the policies that are adopted in the development plan are often amongst the key determinants of the decision made regarding a specific development proposal. In a very real way, by the time it comes to commenting on a specific proposal, it is too late if the policy issues have already been settled in a particular way. This is reflected in the planning legislation itself. Section 34 of the Planning & Development Act 2000, referring to applications for permission to carry out development, states that:

> 'When making its decision in relation to an application under this section, the planning authority shall be restricted to considering the proper planning and sustainable development of the area, regard being had to:
>
> (i) the provisions of the development plan,
>
> (ii) the provisions of any special amenity area order relating to the area,
>
> (iii) any European site or other area prescribed for the purposes of section 10(2)(c),
>
> (iv) where relevant, the policy of the Government, the Minister or any other Minister of the Government,
>
> (v) the matters referred to in subsection (4), and
>
> (vi) any other relevant provision or requirement of this Act, and any regulations made thereunder.'

From this, it is clear that the decisions of the planning authority are very policy-related and that the development plan is one of the key policy documents that determine these decisions. Citizen participation in the making of these policies, therefore, is a critical element in facilitating input into the making of the decisions regarding individual developments that the development management system regulates.

Given the importance of the role of the development plan and the generally-accepted fact that citizen participation in the development plan-making process is far less than in the making of decisions regarding specific development proposals, this paper focuses on the opportunities for citizen participation in the development plan-making process.

# The Irish Planning System – The Legal Context

The process for creating and adopting a development plan provides roles for the elected members of the local authorities, for the officials (through the role of the City or County Manager), for specific bodies representing a range of interests (prescribed bodies), and for the general citizen.

The principal steps for making a development plan, as laid down in the legislation, are:

1. The planning authority must publish a notice of its intention to make a new development plan for its area:

   ◊ This notice is sent to certain bodies and also published in the newspapers.

   ◊ The notice invites submissions from those being consulted, including the general public, as to the issues that should be addressed in the development plan.

   ◊ The local authority must also consult with providers of services in the area regarding their plans.

   ◊ The notice must also state where and how background papers are available.

2. The legislation specifically says that:

   '(3)(a) As soon as may be after giving notice under this section of its intention to review a development plan and to prepare a new development plan, a planning authority shall take whatever additional measures it considers necessary to consult with the general public and other interested bodies.

   (b) Without prejudice to the generality of paragraph (a), a planning authority shall hold public meetings and seek written submissions regarding all or any aspect of the proposed development plan and may invite oral submissions to be made to the planning authority regarding the plan.'

3. The city/county manager must prepare a report for the elected members regarding the submissions received and the outcome

of any other complications and must make recommendations to the elected members as to how these issues should be addressed.

4. Having considered the report, the elected members can direct the manager as to how certain matters are to be addressed in the development plan.

5. The manager then arranges for a draft development plan to be prepared and presented to the elected members.

6. The elected members may adopt or amend the draft development plan.

7. The draft development plan is put on public display and observations requested from the general public and prescribed bodies.

8. The manager must prepare a report on such submissions for the elected members and make recommendations as to how such submissions should be addressed and whether the draft development plan should or should not be amended.

9. The elected members may adopt the draft plan as the development plan or adopt an amended version of the plan.

One other feature of the legislation to note is that the 2000 Act specifically states that:

'(15) When considering the draft development plan, or amendments thereto, a planning authority may invite such persons as it considers appropriate to make oral submissions regarding such plan or amendment.'

From this, it can be seen that there are roles for the elected members who adopt the plan and give directions to the manager, for the manager (and, by implication, his/her staff) in assessing submissions, making proposals and preparing drafts, for representative bodies in their being specifically contacted and consulted, and for the general public in being given an opportunity to make submissions and observations. It is also clear that the legislation intends that the process be participatory and consultative.

While the legislation may provide opportunities for such participation and consultation, however, it does not prescribe the precise mechanisms that must be used, beyond the giving of public notice regarding the various stages of the plan-making process. Ultimately, the legislation is minimalist in what it requires, while being quite expansive in what it permits. The extent to which participation and consultation takes place, therefore, to some extent at least, will be determined by the model of planning and policy-making that is adopted by the planning authority.

## THE IRISH PLANNING SYSTEM – THE POLICY CONTEXT

At about the same time that Arnstein was publishing her work, the issue of public participation in the planning process was being considered in the United Kingdom. This was exemplified by the *Report of the Committee on Public Participation in Planning*, known as the Skeffington Report (1969), produced on behalf of the Ministry of Housing & Local Government. As noted by the Royal Town Planning Institute:

'That report accepted the need to involve the public in planning, and made far-reaching recommendations which influenced subsequent legislation in the early 1970s. Publicity and consultation became required components of the statutory planning system, providing local people with opportunities to comment on, and object to, development plans and planning applications. Planners in the 1970s embraced this new responsibility with some enthusiasm, and time and effort was spent preparing exhibitions and organising public meetings. Despite the enthusiasm, the response from the public was typically disappointing. Gradually, this led many councils to reassess their commitment to public consultation and to carry out only the minimum necessary to meet the requirements of the planning acts.' (Illsley, 2002)

It might be argued, of course, that while this process referred to 'participation', it was, in fact, more akin to a process of consultation. More recently, the UK Government published a report titled, *Participatory Planning for Sustainable Communities* (ODPM, 2003). This report contains a range of recommendations, which, if adopted, will result in a more participatory rather than consultative approach to planning in the UK.

Interestingly, perhaps, the issue of public participation in Irish land-use policy-making has not been addressed by policy-makers in the Republic of Ireland in the same way as it has in the UK. Thus, there is no equivalent to the Skeffington Report (1969), or the report *Community Involvement in Planning: The Government's Objectives* (ODPM, 2004). Nor, indeed, have Ministerial Guidelines been issued that deal specifically with this matter. Though referred to in the recently-issued *Development Plans: Guidelines for Planning Authorities* (DoEHLG, 2007), the references are both limited and in the form of exhortation rather than a requirement:

> 'Councils should also actively involve citizens in the whole process of making the plan, especially those who may not normally contribute or engage in the process. Councils *should consider* [italics added] innovative methods to encourage as wide a public consultation as possible. It is vital that, from an early stage, as much public and political consensus is built around the strategic direction the new plan is to take.' (DoEHLG, 2007, p. 56)

It is possible to speculate on a number of reasons why this might be so. In the first instance, it is possible that it is considered that the legislation is adequate in providing the opportunities for participation. It is also possible that the smaller-scale nature of Irish local government, and the clientelist nature of its political processes, have limited the perceived need for such statements. It is also plausible to suggest that the establishment of Strategic Policy Committees within local authorities, with their combined elected member/community membership, may have encouraged the idea that the need for public engagement in plan-making was satisfied and that little further was required.

With regard to policy requirements, while there is no great national policy imperative requiring that planning decision-making be pursued in a collaborative way, neither is there any particular policy position that would be opposed to it. If anything, there is at present a positive attitude towards participatory structures and collaborative processes.

Indeed, as noted by Callanan:

'The partnership process at national level is generally credited with providing a stable industrial environment, and being one of the contributory factors for economic growth during the 1990s.' (Callanan, 2003, p. 4)

The same author:

'... has noted a number of policy documents from central government stressing the importance of encouraging greater ownership of, and participation in local decision-making. These include:

◊ *Better Local Government* (DoE, 1996).

◊ *Report of the Task Force on the Integration of Local Government & Local Development Systems* (DoELG, 1998).

◊ *Preparing the Ground: Guidelines for the Progress from Strategy Groups to the County/City Development Boards* (DoELG, 1999).

◊ *A Shared Vision for County/City Development Boards: Guidelines for the CDB Strategies for Economic, Social & Cultural Development* (DoELG, 2000).

◊ *Towards Sustainable Local Communities: Guidelines on Local Agenda 21* (DoELG, 2001).' (Callanan, 2003, pp 7-8)

There is, therefore, the basis of a policy agenda that looks to partnership and collaboration, even if this has not been specifically articulated for the land-use policy-making process. Again, however, the policy context will not determine the place on the participation ladder that the process will occupy. It facilitates but does not prescribe.

## The Irish Planning System –
## The Institutional Context

Very little work has been done in analysing the mechanisms used in the making of development plans in Ireland. Using the models proposed by Innes & Booher, outlined in **Chapter 1**, it is suggested that the approaches that have been adopted in Ireland to the preparation of development plans have reflected the 'technical/bureaucratic' model and the 'political influence' model. This is reflected in the comments of Callanan above, and can also be seen in various comments from politicians and others about the lack of engagement by local authorities, and particularly by local officials, with stakeholders in the process.

It is understandable, perhaps, why these are the models that have been followed. The planning system was established in the 1960s, at a time when Irish society was relatively homogenous, when there was little understanding of the interdependencies between interests, when there was not a great diversity of interests perceived, and when the interests of the powerful were considered to be coterminous with the interests of society. This is reflected in the integrationist tendency of community and other organisations at the time. As noted by Curtin & Varley:

> 'Epitomised in Ireland by the representative Community Councils of *Muintir na Tíre*, the integrationist tendency is remarkable for an "all-together" ideology that projects itself as concerned with the common good and as capable of transcending class, party, gender, religious and even spatial divisions within localities.' (Curtin & Varley, 1997, p.379)

Thus, at the time that the culture of planning was being established in Ireland, the conditions existed that Innes & Booher suggest as being supportive of the technical/bureaucratic model. Writing in 1983, Komito stated that:

> 'In contrast to most Western European states, differences in occupation, social class, region, or religion are neither salient political issues nor the basis of party cleavages.' (Komito, 1983)

In addition, the complexity, technical nature and scale of the processes involved, as well as the emergence of a cadre of professional planners, which was committed to a professional ethic that was expert-based and independent of community perspectives, tended to emphasise the role of the technical and bureaucratic elements of the process. While elected members from time to time sought to become engaged in the process, their limited technical capacity and their limited understanding of the complex context within which the development plan had to be prepared compromised their capacity to engage fully at a technical or policy level. The elected members, therefore, tended to address policy issues from a clientelist perspective, which tended to generate the political influence elements of the Irish approach. This approach reflected the way in which local government and, indeed Irish political life in general, tended to operate:

'Ireland's traditional political culture of clientelism means that individual citizens regularly approach elected representatives, at both national and local level, for assistance in their dealings with public bodies.' (Callanan, 2003, p 3).

Thus, the expectations of the general public, the elected members and, indeed, the public officials, tended to give rise to a process within which the elected members dealt with the officials on an adversarial basis, which was resolved through the mechanisms of the political influence model:

'During the course of the five-yearly revision of the County Development Plan, it has become clear that this too has become merely another means by which councillors can facilitate individuals with specific interests. Whatever policy functions are being exercised during the review, there are also pieces of land being rezoned without reference to overall plans. When councillors change the zoning of particular pieces of land, it is often on the basis of representations by those who own the land.' (Komito, 1983)

In addition, the particular role of the City/County Manager within the Irish local government system (with a personal authority deriving from statute, and not delegated to him/her by the elected members) gives individual managers a quasi-political mediation role, in which they often seek to create a complementarity of interests that could be used to generate agreed policies. Often, the interest of the manager was in seeing a policy adopted that was acceptable to the elected members and that was not *ultra vires*. This political expediency approach often brought the manager into conflict with the technical planning specialists in the local authority and aligned the role of the manager more with that of the elected members of the local authority than with the staff. Writing of Ireland, admittedly in 1983, Komito stated that:

> 'To a great extent, bureaucrats assist politicians because they gain more by permitting politicians' activities than by preventing them. In exchange for responding to politicians' representations, bureaucrats are able to retain their independence on substantive matters of policy and administration.' (Komito, 1983)

Thus, within the Irish system, it can be argued that, as time went on, a struggle has emerged between the technical/bureaucratic model as espoused by the planners and the political influence model as used by the City/County Manager and the elected members, and that this struggle still goes on, though it has been significantly modified in recent times. It is suggested that this struggle can be further ameliorated by a more collaborative approach, in which the participants share their interests and visions and seek the common ground that undoubtedly exists.

# 8

# PARTICIPATION, POLITICS & ORGANISATIONS

## *Paul Keating*

In this chapter, we will look specifically at the implication and challenges of participatory planning process for institutions, most particularly State agencies such as the local authorities. This issue goes to the heart of the relationship between the State and its citizens and the extent to which State institutions have the capacity to engage meaningfully and to respond in an integrated way to the IAP process.

We will look briefly at the politics and ideologies of participatory development and planning, the values associated with such ideologies and the importance of such values for individuals, teams and organisations engaging with the IAP process.

The sustainability of participatory planning processes and their capacity to effect significant change is dependent on the extent to which they are absorbed by institutions. The *institutionalisation of participation* is the central theme of this chapter. This concept will be examined from the perspective of the internal culture of the organisation itself (intra-organisational participation), the capacity of the organisation to engage in meaningful partnership (inter-organisational participation) and the broader issue of active citizenship and State agencies (citizen participation).

There is emerging a broadly-based recognition of the need on the part of State agencies to engage more actively with citizens. There are many progressive and well-tested models of organisational development that facilitate participatory management. The potential of the IAP process in Ireland may not be to stimulate the radical social change advocated by many proponents of participatory development but with other similar methodologies, to provide a constructive and structured means by which citizens can engage in a meaningful way with State agencies.

This chapter concludes that the next phase in the application of participatory planning needs to involve a consolidation of methodologies and the institutionalisation of such approaches into the workings of local authorities and other State agencies. In addition to clear methodologies, such a development would need continued organisational and legal reform, as well as substantial capacity-building at community and organisational level.

# THE POLITICAL CONTEXT OF PARTICIPATION

In the context of participation, the emphasis of many global development practitioners and social thinkers in Europe is on the potential of participatory development to facilitate inclusion, on one hand, and fundamental social change, on the other. This reflects a broader debate within development theory, which appears to be fragmented between the traditional theories of economic and social modernisation and those presenting a more radical perspective on underdevelopment and sustainable economics.

## Political and development theory

The contrasting positions relating to development are also manifest in political theory. Communitarianism provides an analysis of citizen governance, based on a delegation of the maximum amount of power to community level. Indeed, authors such as Hirst (2000) would argue that there is a real need to develop an understanding of the political analysis of participation in order to avoid a superficial 'managerial' and, at times, coercive application of participation by large organisations. Callanan (2002) presents a conceptual framework that juxtaposes the liberal/managerial approach with the communitarian approach. The former he describes as 'benevolent paternalism':

'... since the participatory mechanisms are not intended to result in any real shift of power between local authorities and citizens.'

On the other hand, the communitarian approach implies a belief in the value of two-way communication for its own sake, and the possibility (or ideal) of reaching a consensus and engendering a greater common identity. In principle, according to communitarian principles, decision-making should be open and accessible to all.

Cooke & Kothari (2001) provide a critique of participation, which articulates the often-cited concern that participatory language and techniques have been 'abused' by those uncommitted to the philosophy of participation, by simply contracting 'participants' into externally-conceived and controlled projects. There is a view that, in using participatory methodologies without a broader social and political analysis, the practitioner or institution is simply reinforcing the social structure that created the conditions of inequality and exclusion, the precise social ills that the participatory methodologies may be seeking to address:

> 'There is a need, then, for participation to be underpinned by a coherent theoretical understanding of the underlying processes of development. There is also a strategic imperative for participation to remain located within a radical tradition of development theory, as to do otherwise would to be complicit in finally emptying the concept of its transformative potential.' (Cooke & Kothari, 2001)

Gaventa (2002) highlights the potential of participation in local governance to re-define and deepen the meaning of democracy and inclusive citizenship. He points out that there are challenges to ensuring that social justice is kept at the centre of this movement and that it is not co-opted for less progressive goals. Power and the renegotiation of power relationships are, as he puts it:

> '… critical to developing an understanding and promoting both participatory democracy and participatory development, for theorists and practitioners alike." (Gaventa, 2002)

Fung & Wright (2003), in arguing for empowered participatory democracy, call for:

> '… the redesigning of democratic institutions so as to incorporate innovations that elicit the energy and influence of ordinary

people, often drawn from the lowest strata of society in the solution of problems that plague them'.

In its guidelines for the Local Development & Social Inclusion Programme, Pobal (1999) identifies the development of active citizenship as a key objective of its approach to community development.

Considerable research is being undertaken on the role of participatory planning mechanisms in fostering more inclusive and deliberative forms of engagement between the citizen and the State. Goetz & Gaventa (2001) argue that these processes may be seen along a continuum, ranging from ways of strengthening 'voice', while also strengthening receptivity to that 'voice' by institutions. They argue that the 'voice', or community, end of the spectrum begins with awareness-raising and building the capacity to mobilise. Sound mechanisms or processes, in themselves, will not guarantee participation. They go on to suggest that strategies should be developed, through which citizens' voices can be heard within the governance process. The strategies they suggest are similar to those advocated in Integrated Area Planning (IAP).

## Participatory development in Ireland

The emphasis on participatory development has been echoed by many development organisations and initiatives here in Ireland. Over the past two decades, social partnership has become a well-embedded concept in both public policy and consciousness in Ireland. The participation of local communities as active agents in the regeneration of their own areas has seen them become partners with statutory agencies and the traditional social partners in developing integrated, multi-dimensional and area-based programmes. Since the early 1990s, these local area-based partnerships have become an established mechanism for promoting popular participation in local development. Whether established by State agencies or as a result of EU initiatives, fora such as LEADER, Area-Based Partnerships, County Development Boards and issue-based committees bring together community, sectoral and institutional representation. These initiatives see themselves as providing a mechanism for participation in decision-making and often provide different ideological perspectives on what participation seeks to achieve. Those organisations coming from a social action perspective, with a specific remit related to poverty and social exclusion, often see meaningful participation by marginalized groups as both a necessary mechanism for addressing these issues and as a measure of success in so doing.

The Community Workers Co-operative (CWC) and the Combat Poverty Agency have been resolute advocates of the need to develop and resource structures in order to ensure effective participation. In 2000, the CWC stated that:

'... in tackling social exclusion, embracing participatory democracy and involving local communities, the development of new and innovative processes will inevitably have to be a central feature ...' (CWC, 2000a).

Since the publication of *Better Local Government* (DoE, 1996), a stated objective of which was the establishment of new participative structures allowing for the involvement of identified interests in the policy-making process, there have been significant changes in the relationship between participative and representative democracy at local level in Ireland. A series of policy documents, stressing the importance of participation in decision-making, has been published by the Department of Environment & Local Government, perhaps culminating in section 127 of the Local Government Act 2001, which provides that local authorities take steps as necessary:

'... to consult with and promote effective participation by the local community in local government'.

The establishment and operation of County Development Boards and Strategic Policy Committees has seen mixed results, as reported by Callanan's review of the SPC structures (2003), where he highlights some of the challenges faced by local authorities and social partners in promoting public participation. In addition to highlighting the achievements of these structures in building relationships and mutual understanding, he makes the point that:

'There is a danger that the most marginalised in society are not heard through participatory mechanisms. Those who shout loudest and whose voice is heard may not always be the most representative – although many often assume otherwise.'

In a detailed analysis of populism of partnership in the West of Ireland, Varley & Curtin (2004) raise the possibility that such initiatives have seen:

'... the State turning some of these community interests into service providers, largely on its own terms'.

The interface between community groups and State agencies is often most apparent through the planning process. With an increased desire, and in some cases requirement, to support public participation in planning, and with heightened capacity and expectations on the part of community-based organisations, attention is now being turned to more structural issues, such as participatory planning processes and institutions' capacity to absorb such processes into their decision-making. Speaking of the capacity of State agencies internationally to engage in a structured way with participatory processes, Khanya (1999) makes the point that:

'There is a lack of capacity at all levels of government in normative planning, which places the emphasis on considered judgement and the discretion of decision-makers, as opposed to the application of standardised rules and regulations. This is also true for participatory planning approaches and ways of addressing poverty.'(Khanya, 1999)

The CWC highlighted many of the challenges it saw as facing State institutions and their staff, including the development of:

'... different and more participative planning techniques'. (CWC, 2000)

## Politics, ideology, values and IAP

'Participation' in a development context is a word loaded with meaning, backed up by bodies of research, conflicting theories and personal and organisational ideologies. This ensures that, while participation is seen universally as being desirable, there are conflicting understandings of its meaning and objectives. The need to achieve a shared understanding of the ideology underpinning the process in which people are being invited to participate cannot be over-emphasised. It goes to the heart of participants' and institutions' expectations and commitment and the varying criteria by which a development process such as the IAP can be judged successful or otherwise.

It seems reasonable to suggest that there will always be this tension between a conservative and a radical approach to development. In Ireland, this tension is apparent at national level through social partnership, at regional level through the various partnership fora, and locally it often manifests itself indirectly through public processes of consultation such as IAP. One of the first, and indeed ongoing, challenges of the IAP process described in this publication was the negotiation of its underlying values among the Tipperary Institute (TI) team facilitating it. Within the IAP team, there is a range of positions and expectations as to the role and potential of participation. This necessitated ongoing clarification of values for individuals and the group. The negotiation of the principles of the IAP, as outlined by Catherine Corcoran in **Chapter 2**, was a critical phase in consolidating the team and developing a shared position. This is not to say that absolute consensus was achieved, or even that it would have been desirable. However, IAP team members need to be given the opportunity to articulate their values and to agree shared principles.

This diversity of values and approach, which at times seemed a liability, in fact was a strength. It was reflected in the different expectations of community members and institutions with which the team engaged. It does not seem unreasonable to assume that an overly homogenous, or fundamentalist, approach on the part of the team could have alienated key stakeholders from the offset and undermined the inclusivity the process was seeking to achieve.

It is not unreasonable to conclude that the conservative position of State institutions in Ireland has been changing in recent years and that structures for participation, unimaginable 20 years ago, have been adopted. However, it should also be pointed out that there is an ever-present demand on the part of elements within the community/ voluntary sector for more meaningful processes for inclusion. These positions could be said to reflect different understandings of the objectives of participation as highlighted in the previous section. Participatory planning can be seen as an important mechanism for achieving inclusion, while the capacity of State institutions to engage with participatory development processes is a key factor in their potential to redefine the relationship between planning authorities and communities.

# THE INSTITUTIONALISATION OF PARTICIPATION

The concept of the *institutionalisation of participation* emerged in the 1990s in response to the experience of community groups and non-governmental organisations (NGOs) in developing countries, when they were faced with the inability of State agencies to engage with, or follow through, on grass roots development initiatives. The term has also come to reflect a development objective, whereby State agencies themselves become participatory organisations and, in turn, become agents for transformative development within their spheres of influence, thus handing institutional leadership from NGOs to statutory agencies.

> 'The scaling up of participation to include more people and places constantly challenges these large organisations to become flexible, innovative and transparent. More specifically, the emphasis on diversity, decentralisation and devolution of decision-making powers ... implies procedures and organisational cultures which do not impose "participation" from above through bureaucratic and standardised practices.' (IIED, 2000)

## The challenge for institutions in "sharing the stick"

Generally speaking, the institutionalization of participation faces a number of challenges. These start at a strategic level, where State agencies with responsibility for local development have been given the role and responsibility as being the *sole* decision maker. Historically, legislation, policies and procedures reinforce this role. Co-operation between agencies has a history of being about delineation rather than about integration. Professionals within State agencies find it difficult to hand over power or "hand over the stick", as Robert Chambers puts it (Chambers, 1998).

Based on international research, Thompson notes that:

> 'Public agencies soon encounter the thorny problem of how to build internal capacity in participatory process-driven approaches without fundamentally changing their cumbersome bureaucratic systems and risk-averse management systems'. (1995, pp.1522-3)

Eventually, he claims, this contradiction can force the agencies either to abandon participatory methodologies (sometimes, while continuing to use the associated rhetoric) or to begin the challenging task of re-orientating their institutional policies, procedures and norms.

There are also a number of interesting points raised by Beauchamp & Dionne with regard to the ability of local authorities in the UK to adapt to more participatory processes (1997, pp.112-118). These included the need for continuity, and for processes to be institutionalised, rather than simply occurring on a 'once-off' basis. Their study also highlights the frequently very high financial costs of consultation and participation, and the opposition from professional bureaucracy to increased participation, as significant challenges. Callanan (2002) maintains that these issues are equally relevant in an Irish context, when evaluating the performance of Strategic Policy Committees, in particular.

This said, there are a number of structural changes, as well as national policy initiatives here in Ireland, that seek to encourage a more participatory and inclusive approach on the part of State agencies:

> 'There is a shared commitment by both the State and the voluntary sector to ensure the involvement of consumers and people who avail of services in the planning, delivery, management and evaluation of policy and programmes. This applies at all levels: national, regional and local.' (DoCRGA, 2000)

Some commentators, such as Catherine Forde from UCC (Forde, 2005), suggest that the new structures adopted by the local authorities are indicative of a top-down approach to development, both in their inception and their implementation. She goes further and concludes that State agencies' interaction with their 'clients' is informed by a 'contractualist and consumerist trend' within the State sector, which, while facilitating closer relationships with the private sector, has created a conflict of cultures and objectives with respect to the community and voluntary sector.

> 'The problem with this consumerist approach is that it is "top-down" and individualist in nature and thus conflicts with a participatory approach, which is by definition "bottom-up" and collective.' (Forde, 2005)

The danger that partnership benefits the State more than the community sector has been presented by O'Carroll:

> 'The emphasis on partnership at all levels, on nation and, ironically, on community, is shown to contribute more to the legitimation of the State than to the cause of community development.' (O'Carroll, 2002)

The IAP process, as described in detail in this book, is a mechanism by which participation can begin to be institutionalised. The challenges for organisations, such as the local authorities, relate to their willingness and capacity to engage meaningfully in participatory processes and to respond effectively to their outcomes.

## Redefining organisational relationships

Broadly speaking, there are three sets of relationships that should be examined when reviewing the commitment of institutions to participation. We can look internally at the culture and decision-making structures within an organisation and see the extent to which these facilitate the participation of their own members in initiating and managing change ('intra-organisational participation'). Secondly, institutions can be evaluated on their ability to absorb the needs and priorities of other organisations with whom they work in partnership ('inter-organisational participation). And, thirdly, we can look at the processes in place to facilitate community or 'citizen participation'.

This suggests that the foundation of a participatory organisation relates initially to constructive internal participatory relationships, which then are built upon by inter-organisational relationships, or partnerships, which in turn facilitate positive participatory relationships with the community.

### Intra-organisational participation

There are particular challenges for hierarchical organisations in becoming the facilitators or implementers of participatory development. The term 'congruence' is used in organisational theory to describe the convergence of one's personal values with those of the organisation within which one works (Barry, 1993). It is seen as being an important factor in organisational effectiveness and job satisfaction for employees.

More recently, the term is being used to describe the congruence between the values and visions of development organisations and the internal practices of the organisations themselves. Crowley (1996) reinforces this point, when he says:

'It is important to keep in mind that organisational structures are not neutral or value-free, …'

He goes on to challenge organisations within the voluntary sector to build institutions that reflect a commitment to:

'… participation, collective interests and solidarity'.

In her study of NGOs in Northern Ireland, Corcoran-Tindill (2002) finds:

'… the organisations studied mainly still operate within … traditional, dualistic modes of power and structures, which are reflected in altruistic approaches to development. Understandings of the types of power, for the most part, were mainly limited to conventional power, *i.e.* "power over". Participatory and relational concepts in use have not actually touched the internal practice of organisations and individuals, therefore, in any significant way.'

Integrated planning at community level inevitably highlights a range of needs, solutions and interventions that cut across the responsibilities of different organisations, as well as across the sub-functions within larger agencies, such as a local authority. Therefore, in order to respond in an effective way to an integrated planning process, support agencies need to have an institutional understanding and commitment to participation, and they need to have the capacity to communicate needs internally and to generate an integrated response. This is a challenge that should not be underestimated.

Following the reforms arising from the 1996 White Paper and the Local Government Act 2001, the structures and areas of responsibility within local authorities have changed significantly. While the purpose of much of the reform was to make the institution more accessible and efficient from a local community perspective, it is only when one seeks to implement practical initiatives, such as the IAP, that one sees the extent to which these changes have been effective. A pro-active relationship between the various sections of the local authority and their ability to co-ordinate their response to community-based planning is critical to its potential success.

Our experience of IAP has shown that, rather than there being an institutional commitment to the process, there has generally been an individual, often from the Planning or Community & Enterprise sections, who champions the IAP process within the local authority. The incorporation of the outcomes from the planning process into decision-making and resource allocation may depend on the ability, authority, availability and motivation of that individual. While a champion, or positive leadership, within large organisations is always an important factor in introducing new ideas and approaches, there is a concern that the process can become too dependent on a single individual from a single partner agency.

Indeed, as the process can take a considerable length of time to complete, and several years to mainstream within the organisation, personnel changes can prove to be a major setback. In the long term, this is not sustainable either from a personal or an organisational perspective. It is imperative, therefore, that organisations, such as local authorities, that may want to encourage community participation examine their own internal organisational cultures and adopt an institution-wide understanding and commitment.

In reflecting on the role of institutions in participatory development processes, Chambers (1997) makes the connection between development, change and learning, claiming that the institutional challenge is:

> '… learning how to learn, learning how to change, and learning how to organise and act.'

What is needed, he proposes, is a practical model of participatory management, within which organisations can safely conduct this process. The model that most closely coincides with his view of participatory development is that of the 'learning organisation'.

The theory and practice of participatory management has been presented and debated for many years. It has been seen as a mechanism for empowering organisations and their staff through a structured system of shared decision-making. In recent years, through the work of Senge (1990) and his concept of the 'learning organisation', the benefits of employee participation again has been highlighted. The model developed by the proponents of the learning organisation advocates personal and team learning, both between the employees of the organisation and with the intention of absorbing the knowledge of external stakeholders. It represents a model of organisational structure and culture that could ensure congruence between participatory and partnership aspirations and organisational behaviour.

Organisations that have a genuine commitment to participatory processes should look at their own internal structures and procedures and ensure that they facilitate a shared understanding and an integrated response to the planning process. Such organisations should encourage, but not become over-dependent on, individual champions and should develop a culture of institutional learning, as espoused in management theories such as that presented by Senge (1990).

*Inter-organisational participation*

As mentioned earlier, partnership and intra-organisational co-operation has been a feature of local and national development in Ireland for decades. Within the IAP process, there is also a requirement that the full range of organisations with a mandate and responsibility for local development be involved in initiating, informing and supporting the implementation of the IAP. One of the principles outlined in **Chapter 2** articulates this objective clearly:

> 'The planning process should seek to develop structures for implementation. The process will seek to engage State agencies fully at local and county level in inputting to the plan and taking responsibility for relevant parts of its implementation in partnership with the local community. The planning process should seek to develop clear visions, goals and objectives, with actions clearly linked to the attainment of agreed outcomes.'

In any individual community, it is likely that LEADER, the Local Development Social Inclusion Programme or Partnership, the local authority, FÁS, possibly the local VEC and the HSE outreach centres, all will have plans drawn up for the delivery of their services within that community. On the other hand, it is likely that an IAP will seek to address rural development, social inclusion, local infrastructure and physical planning, education, health and childcare (the respective areas of responsibility of the agencies). It is critical, therefore, that these organisations engage actively with the IAP.

Part of the integration inherent in IAP needs to be an integration of response by State agencies and other organisations to community needs. It is a key element in any IAP that the support of a full range of such organisations be enlisted as part of the process. Not to do so will leave major gaps in the implementation of the IAP. It may mean that:

◊ Relationships with agencies will need to be developed, subsequent to the plan being completed.

◊ There will be substantial gaps in what that IAP can address meaningfully.

◊ Plans will need to be separately tailored for each agency.

None of these scenarios is desirable from a community's perspective.

Based on our experiences, constructive co-operation between agencies in supporting the IAP process can often be one of its greatest challenges. Potential conflict can arise with regard to differing ideologies, varying resources, overlapping mandates, unclear responsibility and differing organisational needs.

It is understandable, and indeed desirable, that organisations come to the IAP process with the intention of addressing their own priorities. However, difficulty often arises when these priorities are not shared and understood by the broader inter-agency group, and where an agency may begin to steer the process in a particular direction, reflecting their needs rather than those of the community. The time to analyse needs, and the possible role of the agencies to support the community in addressing them, is once there is consensus at community level as to what those needs are. Agencies then should assess their capacity to provide such support and should incorporate such responses into their own organisational plans and strategies for the area.

It is not unusual for conflicts to emerge as to the approach an IAP should take. This is often based on an organisation's, or individual's, ideology or approach to development. The dichotomy in the interpretation of the desired outcome of development can create a tension at partnership fora, where organisations coming from differing perspectives sit down to agree on a joint approach to promoting community participation. While the negotiation on personal values, as described previously in this paper, is important and sensitive, negotiation regarding organisational values is doubly so. Some organisations can feel threatened by the possibility that the social inclusion agenda may dominate, and enterprise and service priorities would be sidelined. Similarly, those partners with a commitment to social inclusion often disengage from a process, if they believe its objectives or its methodology will not secure the meaningful participation of those groups usually excluded from such processes. It is important, therefore, that, from the beginning, participants clarify the values that are important to their agencies and accept the validity of other approaches and explore complementarily between them.

While, sometimes, heated negotiations between agencies, and with the community, on roles and responsibilities in supporting the outcomes of the planning process are inevitable, the absence of clarity with respect to a framework for this negotiation can lead to conflict between agencies which, in turn, can lead to major delays, and/or a range of potential supports being withdrawn or overlooked. This can prove very frustrating for the community, as they may see such delays or omissions as indicating a lack of, or indeed withdrawal of, support on the part of the agencies at the critical stage in the process, once the plan has been compiled and its implementation is being considered.

In order to ensure a good working relationship between agencies, and to facilitate a constructive collective response to the plan as it emerges from the community, there needs to be clarity from the outset as to the roles, resources and responsibilities of the different agencies with respect to the process. There should also be a discussion as to what the agencies themselves want from the process and how they are in a position to respond to its outcomes. In this way, the agencies themselves should become considered advocates for the plan and actively seek solutions to the needs identified by the community.

## Citizen participation

The emphasis being placed on citizen participation *vis-à-vis* local governance is a global phenomena that resonates very clearly in Ireland. This emphasis may be motivated by a desire to address dysfunctional structures for local government and development, or as a result of a perceived weakening in the relationship between citizens and their state. In many established democracies, traditional forms of political participation are in decline, and several recent studies highlight the distrust citizens have of many state institutions. In the UK, for instance, a study sponsored by the Joseph Rowntree Foundation points to the need to build a new relationship between local government and local people. The study suggests that the reason for this is a feeling of public alienation and apathy towards local government which the authors conclude:

> '... is a symptom of a deeper malaise, the weakness or lack of public commitment to local democracy.' (Clarke & Stewart, 1998)

Declining participation in the electoral process has also become a cause of concern in Ireland. The fact that local government is at a more distant remove from communities than in most western democracies means that such a decline has more significance with respect to the relationship between the citizen and the state than is the case elsewhere. For example, in France, Germany and the United States of America, representative politics has its roots at local community level. This 'democratic deficit' in the past has been made up by a high degree of participation by Irish people in community and voluntary activity. In recent years, we have experienced a significant decline in popular participation in such voluntary activity and a change of identity for the community voluntary sector, as a result of the proliferation of partnership between the state and civil society.

The establishment of the Taskforce on Active Citizenship highlights the concern felt at senior political levels about the weakening relationship between citizens and the state. In introducing the recently published Report of the Taskforce (2007), An Taoiseach, Bertie Ahern, commends the taskforce for presenting recommendations that will:

> '... assist the Government and other stakeholders in promoting a continued sense of community and greater engagement with civic and democratic processes.' (Taskforce on Active Citizenship, 2007)

The taskforce itself defined 'active citizenship' as processes that enable:

> '... people engage in the political and decision-making process at various levels; how well they are informed or enabled to be active and how various groups can be effectively included.' (Taskforce on Active Citizenship, 2007)

The taskforce's report presents a wide range of recommendations, strongly advocating engagement by citizens but also highlighting the need for State agencies to become more open to citizen participation in decision-making. This emphasis on the mechanisms for participation is also highlighted in an extensive study of international local government decision-making processes undertaken by McGee *et al.* (2003). The authors examine the extent to which citizens participate and conclude that two broad issues need to be addressed:

◊   The legal framework to facilitate citizen participation.

◊   The creation of the culture and the capacity within the State and political establishment to enable local participation in decision-making.

In its County Development Strategy for 2002-2012, Waterford County Council (2002) states its commitment to '… empowerment and participation, to achieve full citizenship, equity and equality …' for all people living in Waterford. A clear link is being established between participation by the local community in the activities of the local authority and active citizenship.

Citizen participation can be seen, therefore, as a necessary mechanism for developing more effective development programmes and renewing confidence in the institutions of the State. It can also be argued that participation can have a more profound objective – that of strengthening local democratic systems and consolidating the relationship between the citizen and the State.

## CONCLUSION

In reviewing the research and the analysis nationally and internationally, one can conclude that there is reason for concern regarding the weakening relationship between citizens and the State. We are challenged to develop the political and popular commitment to meaningful participation that would seek to address this. Internationally, considerable emphasis is placed on the potential of participatory methodologies to stimulate, and indeed consolidate, radical social change and to address the issues of social inclusion and equality. The IAP process presented in this publication does not seek to go beyond the ambition of collaborative planning and facilitating community participation. This ambition, however, could achieve a profound change in the relationship between State agencies and citizens if the IAP model were adopted as a universal approach to local planning on the part of the local authorities. Such a move would require the radical institutional change described in this paper and the investment in time and training to make it possible. A new relationship would be built between local authorities and communities that would not only make for more effective community plans but could mobilize citizen participation, promote social inclusion and strengthen the democratic system itself.

While there may be the potential for institutional transformation of the scale described, it is likely to be a slow and uncertain process, if it is to move in that direction at all. There is, undoubtedly, a populist political call for active citizenship and institutional reform, however the momentum for change 'on the ground' seems to have slowed and the commitment to recreating models of partnership, as happened in the 1980s and 1990s, seems less urgent.

The thesis being presented in this paper is drawn from a limited range of national and international research on the subjects of development, political systems, governance and participatory planning. This is also supplemented with a range of experiences in interacting with institutions undertaking or considering participatory planning approaches. This study is by no means conclusive and highlights the need for further research here in Ireland into the potential of participatory planning to facilitate institutions of the State to engage genuinely in an inclusive and integrated way with community. There is an underlying assumption that there is a willingness on the part of institutions to seek such an engagement. This needs to be tested and analysis undertaken as to how such values are absorbed into the culture of State institutions and, ultimately, how the positive rhetoric of active citizenship can be applied in practice.

# 9

# SOCIAL INCLUSION *vs* SOCIAL INTEGRATION

## *Cora Horgan*

'Community development is most effective when set in the context of an integrated development strategy, which recognises the connection between the social, cultural, economic, political and environmental aspects of development and the importance of planning and co-ordination.' (Frazer, 1996, p.269).

Since a process such as Integrated Area Planning (IAP) aims to act as this integrated development strategy, Tipperary Institute defines it as:

'… an empowering, practical and participatory process to collect, analyse and compile information while developing the skills and structures needed to prepare and implement an inclusive and multifaceted plan for a defined geographical area'.

In order to realise this process, the two words 'integrated' and 'inclusive' are essential to the overall realisation of a practical and deliverable plan, which reflects the needs of all members of the community, shaping solutions that improve quality of life for all.

If, according to Curtin (1996), community is a 'means to an end … part of a strategy for mobilising all local actors to solve socio-economic problems', then the issue for a process, such as the IAP in this scenario, is the mobilising of these local actors or groups – identifying who they are, and providing them with the opportunities for becoming not only meaningfully involved, but developing a sense of ownership about both the process and its outcomes. This is where the need to focus on social inclusion and social integration emerge. These two terms share many similarities and, indeed, can be found as interchangeable terms in discussions referring to the combating of social exclusion. This chapter will explore broadly the context of social exclusion, as it exists in rural areas. Such exclusion encompasses issues of spatial and social inequality. A process such as the IAP aims to address rural community development by addressing both types of issues, through combining social inclusion and social integration. By doing so, specific excluded groups within a community are identified and supported, while, at the same time, working through a socially-integrated horizontal community approach that aims to promote the development of the community in its entirety, in a wider context of inadequate service and resource provision.

## THE CONTEXT OF RURAL SOCIAL EXCLUSION

The concept of social exclusion is an attempt to understand poverty in a broader sense and can be said to be a multidimensional state, caused, not just by economic deprivation, but also by social deprivation over a sustained period. An underlying dilemma of the IAP process is how to address such issues of inequalities between social groups within the community and, at the same time, to address the disadvantages or needs that the community as a whole faces. This reflects an ongoing debate in addressing rural social exclusion, which acknowledges the spatial as well as socio-structural causes of social exclusion.

The European Conference on Rural Development, held in Salzburg in 2003, recognised the diversity of rural Europe and stressed that rural areas were suffering from inadequate access to services, alternative employment and opportunities for development. The conference identified the need to ensure that the wider rural community is strengthened, in order to promote sustainable rural development.

This reflects the Irish *White Paper for Rural Development* (Department of Agriculture & Food, 1999), which discusses a rapidly-changing economy during the 1990s, resulting in uneven economic and social development across the country, with an ageing rural population, service concentration in urban centres, declining significance and potential of agriculture as a sector, disproportionate growth in employment in Dublin and the South West and categories, including the unemployed, women, people with a disability, older people, migrants, local authority tenants, travellers, lone parents, Gaeltacht communities, fishermen and farmers on small holdings (NESF, 1997), as having an increased risk of poverty in rural areas.

The *National Anti-Poverty Strategy* (NAPS) is also very clear as to the socio-economic decline that many rural areas are facing, and the need to ensure that there is a strong focus on combating rural disadvantage, identifying the provision of employment and support services, and infrastructure, as well as the empowerment of the local community as being essential to tackling poverty and exclusion in rural areas (Department of Social & Family Affairs, 2003).

The *National Development Plan* (Department of Finance, 1996) identifies contributory factors to exclusion as including limited access to transport, services, poor infrastructure, physical and social isolation, demographic deficits, and higher costs for goods and services. Specific policies have been put in place under the NDP, including the NAPS, the partnership programmes and the establishment of other specific programmes such as RAPID, CLAR and the Local Development Social Inclusion Programme (LDSIP), to tackle social exclusion. Some of these are general programmes, while some have a rural focus. They alone cannot, however, address the real issue of rural social exclusion and, indeed, provide an added concern that they are a 'quick fix' – following their initiation, individuals and communities should then take the responsibility for addressing ongoing exclusion. Instead, such programmes must include a strong animatory and developmental, process-focused, aspect, usually in the form of support workers. This provides for groups and individuals to receive capacity-building supports, both in terms of identifying their needs, solutions and ways to implement these solutions.

The LDSIP demonstrates this developmental support in its implementation, operating through three measures that are:

'... designed to counter disadvantage and to promote equality and social and economic inclusion'. (Pobal, 2006)

These measures – services to the unemployed, community development and community-based youth initiatives – are delivered at local level by 38 Area-based Partnerships, 31 Community Partnerships and two Employment Pacts. A strong element of partnership is built into the programme, reflected by the make-up of boards of directors of these local organisations. So too is animation and capacity-building, with professional development officers working across the multi-annual programme, providing support and sustainable development to groups on an ongoing basis. The existence of professional support workers allows for pre-development and ongoing support that aims to create a sustainable impact beyond the life of the funding itself.

On the other hand, programmes such as CLAR take a different approach, focusing on the actual monetary funding as the key element of support. CLAR:

> '... provides funding and co-funding to Government departments, State agencies and local authorities in accelerating investment in selected priority developments'. (Pobal, 2006)

This approach, which does not provide for complementary support through associated workers, is rather a stop-start approach, addressing pre-identified issues through State and other agencies, and not providing for the ongoing capacity for communities to build up skills and structures to react to needs on a long-term basis.

Approaches to rural disadvantage place a strong focus on spatial disadvantage, and an integrated approach employed to raise the community as a whole in its development, adopting an 'equal opportunity' methodology. Using an objective analysis of distribution of disadvantage certainly highlights rural areas in need of special attention. However, the difficulty with this 'positive territorial discrimination' is that it ignores the hidden disadvantage that exists in all communities, deprived or affluent, falling into:

> '... the trap of thinking of areas as having problems, rather than being places where people experience problems'. (Pringle, 2002)

Individuals, groups and communities experience 'multiple disadvantage' (Department of Agriculture & Food, 1999), with spatial disadvantage exacerbating social inequalities, which are not confined to the most visibly poor rural areas, nor medium and larger towns, but have a significant impact on the lives of a substantial minority of those people living in smaller rural communities, not always as visible due to an absence of critical mass. Their 'invisibility' is a concern, and tackling this 'social group inequality' that includes factors such as class, gender, income, family status, age, disability and ethnicity (Pobal, 2003) without stigmatisation is a necessary prerequisite to addressing rural disadvantage. 'Social exclusion' as a term can be rather open-ended, often identified as a result of a combination of linked problems, and its dispersed presence in rural communities must be addressed in order to achieve social equity – that a person's quality of life is not adversely affected either by their belonging to a particular 'social category' or because of living in a particular area (Dalal-Clayton & Bass, 2002), and each of these categories brings with it its own characteristics and requirements. While social exclusion is most often associated with poverty, there has been a shift in terminology to encompass exclusion from social relations and networks at the local level (Tovey *et al.*, 1996), perhaps due to other factors, including the recent phenomenon seen in rural Ireland of a large influx of newcomers moving into small rural communities that may previously have seen a population decline. Looking at social exclusion from such a wide perspective results in few, if any, communities, rural or urban, in Ireland that do not experience exclusion to some level (Tovey *et al.*, 1996).

In addressing rural social exclusion, it is clear that there is a need to address both spatial and social inequalities. In addressing rural disadvantage and exclusion, addressing the issues of the area or community as a whole is important, harnessing as it does the critical mass of the community as a whole, and employing the 'rising tide lifts all boats' attitude. There must be, however, to continue the analogy, the recognition of differing 'sizes' of these boats or, in other words, a complementary emphasis on inequality *within* rural communities as well as *between* them. The dilemma lies in whether to prioritise one over the other. While there is a case for placing social inequality as a priority before spatial inequality (Pobal, 2003), in terms of addressing rural social exclusion, the IAP process aims to bring a two-pronged approach to addressing exclusion, by employing both social inclusion and social integration, and facilitating communities to develop a cohesive and practical strategy of their own making, accompanied with practical initial strategies for implementation of their IAP.

## SOCIAL INCLUSION

The Centre for Economic & Social Inclusion describes 'social inclusion' as:

> '... the process by which efforts are made to ensure that everyone, regardless of their experiences and circumstances, can achieve their potential in life'. (Britton & Casebourne, 2002).

The *White Paper on Rural Development* defines 'social inclusion' as:

> '... a term linked to addressing the different processes of marginalisation in society. It embraces not only economic factors such as unemployment, poverty and inadequate incomes but also wider social issues of isolation, powerlessness and lack of influence and inequalities in terms of access to decision-making channels.' (Department of Agriculture & Food, 1999)

Access to essential services, participation in local organisations, and interaction within the community are all-important aspects of social inclusion. Social inclusion is the process whereby recognition is made that there are different needs and issues facing different members of the community, and targeted efforts or responses are made to ensure that all have access to opportunities available to the majority, and the capacity to realise these opportunities. Curtin, in Tovey *et al.* (1996), discusses a 'conflict model' of community development that, while favouring collective action, also focuses more directly on marginalised target groups, outside the general community power structures. Pobal, in its study on community work under the LDSIP, proposes:

> '... work which starts with targeting the most excluded in a community will eventually begin to address issues of spatial inequality'. (Pobal, 2003).

This shifts the focus towards inequalities experienced by social groups within spatial communities, focusing on contributory factors of disadvantage, and aiming to provide 'self-expression of people suffering exclusion'. The inclusion of those groups and individuals, who are experiencing social exclusion, allows for the opportunity to identify innovative and relevant solutions to exclusion, and allows for the capitalisation of other local resources (Pringle, 2002).

The multi-dimensional nature of exclusion has already been highlighted. There is a real challenge to acknowledge this when working with disadvantaged groups. Most studies agree that it is highly desirable to animate a bottom-up approach to inclusion, with the capacity of individuals and groups promoted and supported. However, there is too the realisation that disadvantage is not solely about individual capacity and participation, but also the economic and social environment within which the individual or group is functioning. Spatial inequalities are a contributing factor in themselves to exclusion – for example, poor transport, lack of childcare and other services – and, indeed, many community development or planning initiatives begin with social integration, or spatial inequality, as the motivating factor. Referring back to the conflict model of community development, in his discussion, Curtin (1996) acknowledges that approaches to dealing with social inclusion have become less about empowerment through protest and conflict with power-holders, but through consensus-based partnership, and 'negotiated partnerships' with State agencies. Thus, social inclusion takes into account the external factors, policies and relationships that facilitate inclusion of all within the planning process.

## SOCIAL INTEGRATION

The very name 'integrated area planning' implies that a number of elements – social, economic, cultural and environmental – are being brought together for an area and examined strategically. Integration, as it is referred to within the title of IAP, is multifaceted, bringing together these aforementioned elements, with participation from stakeholders from the community, private and State sectors. Social integration could be seen as the ultimate community-planning scenario; everyone brought together, everyone's needs voiced and placed on an equal playing field, actions to suit these needs and resources being identified to add value towards the greater good. Very much based on a 'whole community approach' (Pobal, 2003) or 'consensus-based approach' (Curtin, 1996), social integration reflects the fact that 'understanding that disadvantage and deprivation tend to be concentrated in particular types of areas' (Commins, 2004), addressing the community's structural limitations, and attempting to address these for the community as a whole. The advantage of adopting a social integration approach is that, for rural communities that are dispersed, it allows the building of critical mass, and identifying core issues, such as infrastructure and services that limit/will benefit the community as a whole. The whole community approach is a ripple approach; by making a basic standard of infrastructure available to all and by initiating development, often by those with stronger social capital, this will eventually motivate development across the community.

Social integration impacts directly on the welfare of all within the community, and is dependant on financial capital, physical capital human capital, public infrastructure and social capital within the community (Piachaud, 2002). While each of these forms of capital vary from individual to individual and group to group, for the purpose of discussing social integration, it is useful to base their definition on the assets of the community as a whole. *Financial capital* is difficult to measure at the community level, relating as it does to assets or resources, rarely in the ownership of the community as a whole. However, the drawing-down of grant aid of some type by a community body or agency within the community may be considered financial capital, as too may fundraising drives, or local authority community funds. *Physical capital* may relate to the property or land in some form of community ownership, either through community councils, associations, the parish structure, etc. *Human capital* relates to the skills and education levels within the community, both in terms of individual participation and in terms of collective action within development and partnership. *Public infrastructure* is the collective services and physical capital that the community has the benefit of. Finally, *social capital* includes norms, networks, rules and social values. Integrating all of these forms of capital is important in order to reduce exclusion, both at the personal and community level. Social capital acts as the cohesive element to social integration, facilitating as it does co-operation within or among groups (Dalal-Clayton & Bass, 2002). Putnam, referenced in Piachaud (2002, p.7), defines social capital as:

'... features of social life ... that enable participants to act together more effectively to pursue shared objectives'.

It is personal, informal, horizontal across the community and sub-group specific. This indicates that, in terms of the process of social inclusion, developing social capital amongst target groups or sectors that experience a common aspect of disadvantage is important, and thus specific activities targeted at these groups are important. However, the process of social integration, horizontal across the community and meeting the needs of the community as a whole, is also important in developing social capital for the community as a whole. In considering the other forms of capital in relation to their ownership by a community, it is likely that they are dispersed in terms of their levels, ownership and accessibility. By working through an integrated methodology, this allows the development of critical mass of such forms of capital, providing a foundation of resources to benefit the community in its entirety.

## IAP: COMBINING SOCIAL INCLUSION & SOCIAL INTEGRATION ... IS THIS SOCIAL COHESION?

Marrying the needs of a disadvantaged area and the needs of disadvantaged or marginalized groups within that area reflects the 'desirability of cohesive societies that respect social differences' (Muddiman, 2000), and poses a challenge for rural community development, whereby spatial disadvantages may be more immediately apparent than social disadvantages. The predicament with social integration is whether it should operate in parallel with social inclusion, or wait until some initial pre-development has been undertaken to empower all sections of the community to participate equally in an integrated process.

There are a variety of approaches to planning and organisation within community development, ranging from the *Muintir na Tíre* model, which has been extremely influential in rural community development over the past number of decades, to models such as the IAP approach to community development, and including the mainstream, area-based approach (through programmes such as LEADER) and the disadvantage-led equality approach (through programmes such as the Local Development Social Inclusion Programme), which all have a similar ethos at their core: helping communities to help themselves. These models, in the past, may have varied in the focus they placed on integration as opposed to inclusion. Approaches that are very much targeted towards working initially primarily with the disadvantaged, it can be argued, come from an urban basis. While rural deprivation is not radically different from urban deprivation, it does need to be responded to in a different way (Tovey *et al.*, 1996).

Co-ordinated targeted inclusion within traditional rural development approaches, including the *Muintir na Tíre* model, have been consensus-based (Curtin, 1996), emphasising the 'whole community' working together with minimum State help, in order to develop strong internal relationships. However, while *Muintir* placed a high emphasis on 'representativeness', in reality, particularly in terms of inclusion, this is difficult to achieve without targeted resources. The past 20 years have seen the burgeoning of a multiplicity of programmes, economic, poverty, social and environmental in focus. These programmes, with strong links to local, national and EU policy, have encouraged communities to tackle poverty and exclusion in partnership with agencies. The current emphasis of decentralisation of decision-making in Ireland to the grass-roots level, being pursued through the organisation of community and voluntary fora through the County Development Board process, while signifying a movement towards a vibrant community sector, still poses challenges to ensuring that all groups and individuals are meaningfully represented and involved and that those community representatives who are participating in larger fora have the legitimacy to speak for their group or community.

In consequence, the organisation of communities and the development of plans and integrated strategies have led to the emergence of models of development, such as the IAP, to support this movement. The challenge facing the IAP process and other models is how to highlight social inclusion as a complementary feature of social integration, to identify the marginalised groups within a community, to support them to identify specific needs and to identify and develop responses to those needs, in the context of developing an socially-integrated development strategy or, in other words, how to undertake a process that results in social cohesion. To answer this challenge, a number of considerations must be borne in mind.

## Identifying stakeholders and understanding their dynamics

To incorporate both inclusion and integration in a process such as the IAP, it is essential to build up a picture of a community in terms of demographic profile, the infrastructure and services of the community and other relevant information. A solid basis of knowledge and information will build a picture of who is in the community, and what the local dynamics are (Pobal, 2003). Different individuals and groups will have differing perceptions of disadvantage within a community, with relativity in terms of neighbours and community members often defining these perceptions. For example, farmers traditionally have been seen as wealthier in Irish rural communities. Yet, smallholders are now defined as disadvantaged. Nonetheless, in the eyes of a low-income family, a smallholder who owns 50 acres may not be 'disadvantaged'. Yet their ability to generate income, and their assets in relation to another farmer, might qualify them as being disadvantaged. Likewise, a dual-income household would not necessarily qualify as being disadvantaged but, if two-hour commuting distances and high childcare costs are taken into account, the household's quality of life may not be as favourable as first appears.

In addition to community stakeholders, the external stakeholders need to be identified and made aware of the process early on; particularly in terms of the added focus and resources required to facilitate social inclusion. These external stakeholders, including local political representatives, external agencies, including local authorities, local development organisations, etc., will have their own agendas that will be affected by the IAP planning process and product. The range of stakeholders involved will have a strong influence on overall social inclusion of the process, as their presence may address the issue of hidden disadvantage, in terms of ensuring that all disadvantaged groups and individuals have a meaningful contribution or are represented in the process, particularly in rural areas where there may be a dispersed pattern of types of disadvantage. For example, a representative of a local development agency working on an equality-based programme (for example, the LDSIP), will have the mandate to monitor the process for a number of marginalised groups. The weighting of representatives in terms of infrastructural development (local enterprise group), area development (County Council) and inclusive development (LDSIP) will have an impact on the overall focus of the IAP. A strong representation on infrastructure and services, with less emphasis on social issues, may result in actions and their implementation being skewed towards the former, due to the mandate of participants in terms of agendas and resources.

Clearly, the process of identifying stakeholders is a challenging one, providing the risk of building exclusion into the overall process from the start, if key groups are not identified. In terms of facilitation of such a process, while working with an additional steering group and other 'gatekeepers' within the community is important, it is unrealistic to expect that this initial steering group will be immediately representative of all community interests, and other desk and field research is needed to build up a clear profile of the resources and stakeholders who will impact and be impacted by the process. By involving the steering group in analysing the profile of the community, and asking it to communicate with other stakeholders, the IAP process may build a clear understanding of both local and external dynamics, particularly as they refer to exclusion. These local dynamics can be invisible, and stakeholders, particularly the original steering group, may be uncomfortable in naming these dynamics. In recognising this, the process builds opportunities for participation and meaningful inclusion, through undertaking pre-development facilitation of target groups, opening membership of task groups, focus groups, sector specific meetings, field survey work, etc.

## Social networks

Focusing on participation and empowerment through a collective approach is an essential feature of community development in tackling poverty and exclusion (CPA, 2000). Three types of social networks have been identified for analytical purposes, evolving from terms that Putnam and others have used in terms of social capital (NESF, 2003):

◊ **Bonding:** Occurs in circumstances where there are strong ties: families, kinship groups, and social groups with a shared identity or interests.

◊ **Bridging:** Connects people and groups with weak ties to different types of people and groups across social and spatial divides.

◊ **Linking:** Connects individuals and groups to others in more powerful positions – for example, between community organisations and statutory bodies.

In terms of bonding and bridging, these two networks can have very different impacts on social inclusion and social integration, with bonding having the potential to create or exacerbate social exclusion, and bridging having the opportunity to increase social inclusion (Muddiman, 2000). Creating or reinforcing strong ties is something that an intense process such as the IAP can result in, particularly if the network involved does not bring new people into the arena. The danger with undertaking a process of social integration without social inclusion is that those people with high social capital and strong capacity are likely to feel more comfortable in either a bonding or linking situation, whereas those coming from an external or weaker point are unlikely to form such close ties. The IAP process may also create a scenario of future exclusion, whereby those not involved in the process may find it difficult, in turn, to become involved in its implementation, both in terms of their own levels of ownership, and also the openness of the network involved in the process. Bridging, on the other hand, brings 'sub-groups', perhaps not previously involved in mainstream community development, particularly the so-called marginalised groups, into the process, building on ties such as shared spatial disadvantage, to create a larger forum for the planning process.

The third social network can be related to the external multi-partnership process that integrated approach will bring. Participatory structures have emerged to the fore in community development in Ireland. The NESC, in setting out principles for developing structures for local development in 1994, stated that the capacity of local groups should be developed to participate in structures for local development, and that strong vertical links from local partnerships to high-level bodies should be developed (NESC, 1994). In order to achieve this, strategic planning and mobilising of local interests must be achieved, through the development, where necessary and not causing duplication, of:

'… a local development coalition of community groups, private interests, State agencies and local government.' (NESC, 1994, p.144)

While they may be representative of an area-based community, the difficulty remains whether they have the capacity and understanding to represent all the interests within that community, not just perhaps their own. In addition to this, the reciprocal relationship between agencies and the community, once seen as 'top-down', also gives an additional linking network to the community, and promotes the breaking-down of barriers between statutory agencies and the community. However, the mandate and power of agency representatives, as well as their own interests and agendas, do much to influence the effectiveness of this partnership both in the integration and inclusion of the IAP. For instance, certain sections within the local authority would be associated, in the main, with capital and infrastructural projects, whereas a local community development group may be more associated with softer supports. Absence of one of these representatives will mean an imbalance in activities and support. In addition, the level of partnership that representatives and agencies commit to also has an impact on the effectiveness of partnership.

*Management and delivery*

Combining social integration and social inclusion in a process such as the IAP creates a testing environment for management within the process, in terms of how to manage the process in general, management of implementation and management of resources, all of which needs to take place for the community as a whole, while ensuring that individual groups and networks within the community are involved.

Managing the IAP process to ensure that it remains true to the community's vision, and allows for everyone to be involved in creating and realising that vision, requires that, not only is the process inclusive, but that objectives and actions relate back to an integrated community vision.

Management of implementation faces the challenge of delivery of actions though participation and inclusion beyond merely representing, by breaking down the plan to a series of discrete projects might result in the overall fundamental vision of integration or aim of the IAP being lost (Mosely *et al.*, 2001) and also the danger of the assumption of a high degree of simplicity and order in the programme cycle, stressing the possibility of following a logical sequence of steps (Cristóvão *et al.*, 1996) by a set number of people.

Management of the process must address this, while also ensuring a spread of actions across the needs of the community, identifying priorities and sequences within those actions, and who within the community has the responsibility for individual actions. There is the tendency in a planning process to allocate lead responsibility to the steering group, 'community council' or specific lead statutory bodies for the majority of actions. This can emerge, either from the overall aim of 'integration' of the IAP to encompass everyone, thus making sense that one body has responsibility for a range of issues, or may also stem from lack of willingness of different groups to take an active role in a specific action, either through lack of resources, fear or lethargy at the end of a long process. Whatever the reason, while this approach may result in integration of the plan, it does not provide for maximum opportunity of participation by a range of people and groups who may previously not have been involved. To counteract this, creating a 'task group' structure aims to build-in maximum inclusion opportunities. Task groups also play an important role in ensuring that a range of actions are delivered in parallel with each other, rather than prioritising actions to take place in a series of discrete projects.

The development of task groups, and naming these groups as having lead responsibility for themes, aims to support social integration. By breaking into smaller groups, this process also facilitates the potential need to place more focus and resources on supporting community members to realise an action, perhaps due to lack of skills or capacity, difficulty in accessing resources or other barriers to inclusion. This mechanism is an important social inclusion tool, allowing individuals to become involved in discrete formats, tackling issues that are of prime interest, often specific activities with named beginnings, middle and end. Not only do these task groups allow actions to be prioritised across a broad range of themes, but they also allow for partnerships to be developed and inclusion of participants to be encompassed, as stakeholders have the opportunity to retain an active role within the implementation process. The development of task groups allows for dissemination of control beyond a small group, reflecting the fear that an 'elitist group' in fact may control the decision-making process, making participation by others meaningless and quickly eroded (Varley, 2006). The evolution of these task groups, from named interests and through the steering group, minimises the danger of co-option onto a structure for the sake of mere demonstration of inclusion. Another challenge facing these task groups is that, once a task group has identified particular actions, there is a natural tendency for those agencies with the mandate or resources to take the lead in delivering them. This, in turn, may disempower other members of the task group, who revert to a 'consultative' role rather than an active role in the delivery of actions that they have been empowered to identify. This is where additional support is required to ensure that participants continue to access support in developing their capacity to play meaningful roles in delivery.

Management of financial, physical, and human capital, resources that are accessed either through local authority sources, local programme/ project sources or through local fundraising, also raises the issue of meaningful participation and inclusion beyond the 'consultation' phase. The vast majority of grant aid now requires a formal structure, often with either charity number or some type of legal entity, or both. In a large number of community settings, there are already legal structures in place, either through the community council or some other larger entity or group. If social exclusion is strongly rooted in power (Commins, 2004; Tovey *et al.*, 1996), then controlling finance or other resources will confer a degree of power on the entity that does so. In tackling social inclusion at the community level, the possibility that 'actors, groups and institutions … collaborate, resist or negotiate new pathways to social inclusion' (Tovey *et al.*, 1996) will reflect the format of these collaborations.

There has been some work done on looking at suitable structures, including the *Muintir na Tíre* model[1], ADOPT model[2], and indeed the

---

[1]    *Muintir na Tíre* was Ireland's premier community development organisation for over 50 years (Curtin, 1996). *Muintir na Tíre*'s approach is based around 'the whole community' as a unit of organisation through which social, economic, cultural and environmental development can take place (www.mnt.ie). *Muintir* aims to develop interaction and relationships within the community, creating a cohesive, mutual infrastructure, with community councils as the representative body, which engaged in projects concerned with a variety of issues in a partnership basis. *Muintir na Tíre*'s relationship with the State supported the development of infrastructure for rural Ireland, ranging from parish halls, schools and sporting amenities to local electrification and group water schemes that were completed far sooner than would otherwise have been the case, with consequent benefits for all involved, through the combination of local voluntary effort with some State money and expertise.

IAP model, also puts forward the steering group, more often in the shape of a reconstituted community council as a potentially overarching legal structure. It is important that identifying such steering groups does not in itself result in a 'top-down' process, once actions and outcomes are identified and responsibilities put in place.

Putting structures in place and accessing resources is dependant on the commitment and capacity of stakeholders, both from community and agency level, to become, and remain, involved. In discussing models of development that are spatial in nature, Varley notes that representativeness counts for little, if the groups involved are ineffective (Varley, 2006). Traditionally, community development groups and associations were relatively independent, relying on a high level of social capital, with high levels of volunteerism allowing for active participation and fundraising, but often from a dominant group of people, with very little input from the marginalised. However, animation of individuals and groups, particularly those traditionally excluded from involvement and decision-making within the local community, supporting them to develop their own capacity and confidence, working with broadly-based groups and agencies to recognise and actively pursue inclusion, requires resources. While it is accepted in general that having a level of social capital within a community prior to its initiation of a planning process such as the IAP, and the building of this social capital is important to the continued

---

2    The ADOPT model is based on five key elements: auditing, planning, organisational development, district development and training. The model is aimed at providing local area-based communities with a framework for participation in community development at local level (Pobal, 2003). The model, pioneered by Ballyhoura Development Ltd, and developed through action research by a team from UCD, aims to tackle the lack of co-operation within the community sector, and weak research and planning by communities who are participating and contributing to local planning and development activities. The ADOPT model assumes a high level of pre-development work and ongoing support from a facilitator, such as a local development group or support worker. ADOPT aims to develop a strong community representative structure, an umbrella group that brings together representatives of the various bodies and groups within the community to ensure that activities are not duplicating each other and that real needs are addressed. This umbrella structure, along with the training and capacity-building that the model promotes, supports communities and their representatives to play a meaningful role in partnership functions with State agencies and other bodies.

application of a plan such as the IAP, Krishna (2001) and Humphreys (2006) suggest that a 'capable agency' is as integral, if not more so, as social capital, in working with disadvantaged communities. It follows that working with disadvantaged groups within a community also requires a 'capable agency' with the resources that this implies in terms of time and finance. This is especially true in aiming to create an inclusive and integrated plan.

In addition to the resources needed to support its development, there are also, of course, the resources needed to deliver the actions identified through the IAP. In combining social inclusion and social integration within the IAP, it is important to point out at this stage that social inclusion as a policy objective, both at national and county level, does have programmes and resources allocated to it, and may result in social inclusion projects accessing greater resources available to them, thus being easier to implement that more broadly-based activities. This, in turn, could negatively impact on a fully integrated delivery. For example, the Local Development Social Inclusion Programme, administered by area-based partnerships and community groups throughout the country, is specifically targeted at countering disadvantage and promoting equality and social and economic inclusion through provision of funding and support.

## Proofing the IAP

The inference of this chapter is that a process such as the IAP should have an impact on every member of the community within which it is taking place, and should be fully representative of that community to be socially integrated. But, in order for the IAP also to be socially inclusive, an assessment of what that impact will be, who it will impact upon most and, indeed, whether that impact is positive or negative, is essential, particularly once the actions and priorities have been identified. If, as previously pointed out, social exclusion can be invisible in rural communities, and social integration assumes equality opportunities for all without active targeting needed, then this issue of impact in terms of positive discrimination for those groups needing additional attention or support to include them in the IAP process becomes ever more important. This is where the area of 'proofing' comes into play.

Proofing, in the context of community development, centres around assessing what impact an action, policy or programme will have on those people termed 'socially excluded'. It aims to ensure that social inclusion is kept at the centre of decision-making. Something frequently done on an *ad hoc* basis, typical proofing mechanisms include:

◊ Assessing the impact of plans on groups experiencing inequality.

◊ Resourcing participation of those affected by inequality, perhaps in terms of accessibility issues, community development mentor, funds contributed by agencies and personnel time.

◊ Focusing attention on social inclusion outcomes, particularly in terms of the level at which they are realised (individual, community, area-based or linking into an external agenda or strategy). It then can be determined whether equality of outcome between marginalised and non-marginalised, in terms of access to and the distribution of benefits from the implementation of the plan, has been realised. (Pobal, 1999)

## CONCLUSION

Social exclusion is multi-dimensional, impacted strongly by spatial, as well as social, disadvantage. Both the social inclusion and social integration approaches to addressing rural disadvantage have strong merit, and combined in a process such as the IAP, develop a methodology to achieve social inclusion/integration of a rural community within a broader developmental context – county, country, policy – to make the community less spatially-excluded. Developing a process such as IAP within a community depends on participation and meaningful involvement of the community as a whole, motivated by both the development of internal leadership and structures, and external support, in terms of time, skills and resources. In order to achieve real social integration, social inclusion is essential and in order to best serve a rural community, due to issues of dispersal and lack of critical mass, social integration is vital in planning a development processes.

A process such as the IAP is different to ongoing development work within a community, wherein targeted responses are developed to address the needs of individual groups. Rather, the IAP process is planning for the whole community – but, to do so, it must have emphasis on those traditionally disenfranchised, in order to represent everyone equally – therefore, social inclusion is essential. Otherwise, it would only be those with high motivation, social capital and capacity who would participate pro-actively in the process, creating a void in what the IAP addresses and missing out on innovative and relevant approaches to problems that address both the community as a whole and the individual concerns and groups within that community.

# 10

## CONCLUSION

### *Ciaran Lynch & Catherine Corcoran*

Collaborative planning, as a theoretical concept, has many strengths in the context of a developmental view of democracy. The approach is based on the viewpoints that:

◊ Stakeholders with different needs and beliefs can agree on actions and programmes from which they can all benefit.

◊ An approach that involves groups working together can provide a greater overall return than the total of that provided by groups working on their own.

◊ Participants can be enlivened by the process and develop networks and relationships that enhance their future effectiveness.

Collaborative approaches to decision-making, as outlined in this book, also have a strong value basis. While there are many techniques available to assist in the implementation of a collaborative approach, these techniques are of little value unless they are used in a context that seeks to enhance the extent of community participation in the decision-making that affects it and which also seeks to include as wide a range of perspectives as possible in that process.

While the theories that underlie collaborative processes are strong (though not uncontested), however their practical application is a very complex matter. The degree of success and failure of any collaborative process is related to a wide range of factors that differ from situation to situation. Indeed, it is unlikely that the precise mix of factors will be the same in any two situations.

This book has reviewed some of the theoretical considerations that underlie collaborative models of planning and has described and analysed a number of practical experiences of the application of a particular planning model in a number of small communities in rural Ireland. It has examined specific aspects of a collaborative approach that seeks to link a particular vision of decision-making to a commitment to sustainable development and its various elements – social, economic and environmental. The Integrated Area Planning (IAP) model used in this approach seeks to bring a variety of decision-makers and stakeholders together into a single process.

While one might accept the theoretical value of a collaborative planning approach, however, one might reasonably wish to examine the extent to which it is effective in practice. The authors of this book believe in the appropriateness of a collaborative approach on the basis of its normative value alone and believe that the development and use of this model is something that should be aspired to within local systems of governance in particular. It is also acknowledged, however, that the implementation of the outcomes of the process is also a critically important issue. Communities that have participated in good faith in an exercise, which has sought to give them influence on the decisions that impact on the way their futures will be shaped, are entitled to feel compromised and disenchanted if the outcomes of that process are ignored by decision-takers, particularly if decision-takers seem to act arbitrarily and without explanation.

Therefore, the extent to which the outcomes of a collaborative planning process are adopted by decision-makers, and the degree of explanation given where the outcomes are not adopted, is a crucial stage in the overall process. The experience of the communities with which Tipperary Institute (TI) has worked over the last eight years in that regard is mixed. Most communities have developed enhanced capacities and purpose within their own members. As a result of these enhanced capacities, new projects and structures have been developed in many communities, some of which have arisen from the process and some of which have existed already but been facilitated by the process.

As noted in other parts of this book, some communities have also seen their principal purposes addressed; have seen specific outcomes proposed in their plans achieved; and have developed an enhanced relationship with at least some of the agencies and bodies that have such a significant impact on their lives.

In other communities, however, the experience at the level of implementation has been less positive. In some cases, the goals and actions that seemed to be agreed in the IAP process were not reflected in formal processes that adopted specific plans and policies; in other cases, decision-makers were perceived to act in ways that seemed to disregard largely the views of the community, as expressed in the community plan; and in other cases, investments fundamental to the future of the communities were not made or were significantly delayed. Where community experiences of a collaborative process are not good, the positive impacts that would be expected from engagement in the process are not merely absent; they can be replaced by negative feelings and the relationships between the community and the agencies and organisations with which they interact can become worse than before. An undelivered expectation gives rise to cynicism and withdrawal and an unwillingness to participate in similar exercises in the future.

It is important, therefore, that a collaborative process be undertaken cautiously and in good faith by all participants. The involvement of 'authoritative actors' becomes extremely important, as does the engagement of all those agencies and organisations that would be involved in the delivery of outcomes that are of importance to the community. A series of goals and outcomes that *cannot* be delivered may be a worse outcome than not engaging in a collaborative process at all.

This highlights the importance of considering issues of implementation of the plan during its preparation and the honest sharing of boundaries by those who will have a say in implementation. It also points to the importance of the participation by key implementation bodies at appropriate points in the collaboration process.

These considerations lead to another important contextual issue that has significant implications for the effectiveness of collaborative processes at local level. Government and governance in Ireland tends to be highly centralised. Many agencies and State organisations are governed by centrally-determined goals, objectives and programmes and have little flexibility to respond to the individual needs of individual communities. This is, in itself, a significant issue but not for full elaboration here. What is important, however, is that the limitations of the flexibility available to agencies and public organisations are made clear during the collaborative process. Honest statement and exploration of boundaries are far more useful and positive than either uncertainty or the giving of an impression that the impossible might be achievable.

Collaborative approaches to planning present significant challenges to existing systems and structures – both formal and informal. Formal structures of decision-making have tended to be expert-led and to be based more in the representative than the participatory forms of Government. A change to a more collaborative approach would:

◊ Challenge power structures at the levels of the community and local government.

◊ Ask experts to adopt a far less prescriptive approach.

◊ Ask politicians to share some of their decision-taking power with lay members of the communities they represent.

◊ Ask existing community leaders to act in ways that reflected the views of the community more than their own personal views.

In addition, a new approach would require changes in:

◊ The education of planners and other professionals.

◊ The resourcing of community organisations and their volunteer leaders.

◊ The relationship between those elected to political office and their constituents.

These are substantial changes to the structures that presently prevail and would require commitment and leadership at the highest levels if they are to be implemented effectively.

This book is a reflection on the experience of a number of attempts to introduce collaborative models of planning into the practices of Irish rural governance. It does not purport to be a definitive statement of practice or of the issues associated with the introduction of such a model. But it is a starting place. It outlines some approaches and issues; it suggests an agenda for further investigation; it identifies possibilities as to how the way decisions are made about small rural communities might be changed; and it identifies some of the benefits as well as the challenges of such approaches. It is hoped that the book will spark further experimentation and debate, and that it will help to focus minds on the need that surely exists to amend the ways in which life-changing decisions that affect a wide range of communities are currently made.

# BIBLIOGRAPHY

Addison & Associates (2004). *Moving towards Excellence in Planning: Regeneration*, London: Planning Officers Society.

Adler, A. (1964). *The Practice & Theory of Individual Psychology*, London: Routledge & Kegan Paul.

ADM – see Area Development Management.

Andaleeb, S.S. & Woford, G.W. (2004). 'Participation in the workplace: Gender perspectives from Bangladesh', *Women in Management Review*, Vol.19, No.1, pp.52-64.

Area Development Management (2003). *Community Work in a Rural Setting: An Examination of Community Work under the Local Development Social Inclusion Programme*, Dublin: Area Development Management.

Arnstein, S.R. (1969). 'A ladder of citizen participation', *Journal of the American Institute of Planners*, Vol. 35, No.4, pp.216-224.

Atherton, G., Hashagen S., Chanan, G., Garret, C. & West, A. (2002). *Involving Local People in Community Planning in Scotland*, London: Community Development Foundation Publications.

Barrow, C.J. (1999). *Environmental Management: Principles & Practice*, London: Routledge.

Barry, Z. & Schmidt, W.H. (1993). 'Values congruence and differences between the interplay of personal and organisational value systems', *Journal of Business Ethics*, Vol.12, No.5.

Bass, S. & Dalal-Clayton, B. (2002). *Sustainable Development Strategies: A Resource Book*, London: International Institute for Environment & Development.

Beauchamp, A. & Dionne, J. (1997). 'Public participation in municipal life: The city of Québec in the North American context', in Pröhl, M. (ed.), *International Strategies & Techniques for Future Local Government: Practical Aspects towards Innovation & Reform*, Gütersloh: Bertelsmann Foundation Publishers.

Belbin, M. (1988). *Team Roles at Work*, Oxford: Butterworth-Heinemann.

Briggs Myers, I., McCaulley, M., Quenck, N. & Hammer, A. (1998). *MBTI Manual – a Guide to the Development & Use of the Myers Briggs Type Indicator*, Palo Alto, CA: Consulting Psychologists Press.

Britton, L. & Casebourne, J. (2002). *Defining Social Inclusion,* London: Centre for Economic & Social Inclusion, available at http://www.cesi.org.uk/docpool/ defsocinc.pdf.

Burton, P. (2003). 'Community involvement in neighbourhood regeneration: stairway to heaven or road to nowhere?', www.neighbourhoodcentre.org.uk.

Callanan, M. (2002). 'The White Paper on governance: The challenge for central and local government', *Administration,* Vol.50, No.1.

Callanan, M. (2003). *Institutionalising Participation & Governance? An Analysis of New Local Government Structures in the Republic of Ireland,* paper to the EUROLOC Network Eighth European Summer School in Local Government, University College Cork, Dublin: Institute of Public Administration.

Carlow County Council (2007). *Hacketstown Local Area Plan,* Carlow: Carlow County Council.

Carr, W. & Kemmis, S. (1986). *Becoming Critical: Education, Knowledge & Action Research,* London: Routledge.

Central Statistics Office (2007). *Census 2006: Principal Demographic Results,* Cork: Central Statistics Office.

Chambers, R. (1997). *Whose Reality Counts? Putting the First Last,* London: Intermediate Technology Publications.

Clarke, T. & Clegg, S.. (1998). *Changing Paradigms: The Transformation of Management Knowledge for the 21st Century,* New York: HarperCollins Business.

Combat Poverty Agency (2000). *The Role of Community Development in Tackling Poverty,* Dublin: Combat Poverty Agency.

Commins, P. (2004). 'Poverty and social exclusion in rural areas: Characteristics, processes and research issues', *Sociologia Ruralis,* Vol.44, No.1.

Community Workers Co-operative (1997). *Strategies to Encourage Participation,* Galway: Community Workers Co-operative.

Community Workers Co-operative (2000a). *Partnership, Participation & Power,* Galway, Community Workers Co-operative.

Community Workers Co-operative (2000b). *Combating Social Exclusion: Identifying the Role & Potential for Local Government,* Galway: Community Workers Co-operative.

Cooke, B. & Kothari, U. (2001). *Participation: The New Tyranny?,* London: Zed Books.

Corcoran-Tindill, M. (2002). *Encouraging Congruent Practice in Irish Development Organisations: Turning the Gaze Back on Ourselves & Asking "What's really going on?",* unpublished MA thesis, Dublin: Kimmage Development Studies Centre.

Covey, S. (1989). *The Seven Habits of Highly Effective People,* New York: Simon & Schuster.

CPA – see Combat Poverty Agency.

Cristóvão, A., Koehnen, T. & Portela, J. (1996). 'Developing and delivering extension programmes' in Burton, E., Swanson, R., Bentz, P. & Sofranko, A.J. (eds.), *Improving Agricultural Extension: A Reference Manual,* Rome: Food & Agriculture Organisation of the United Nations, available at http://www.fao.org/docrep/ W5830E/w5830e09.htm#TopOfPage, accessed 17.1.2008.

Crowley, N. (1996). 'Frameworks for partnership: Merging models and responses', in Curtin, C. (ed.), *Partnership in Action: The Role of Community Development & Partnership in Ireland,* Galway: Community Workers Co-operative.

CSO – see Central Statistics Office.

Curtin, C. & Varley, T. (1997). 'Community action and the State' in Clancy, P., Drudy, S., Lynch, K. & O'Dowd, L. (eds.), *Irish Society: Sociological Perspectives,* Dublin: Institute of Public Administration, p.379-409.

Curtin, C. (1996). 'Back to the future? Communities and rural poverty' in Curtin, C., Haase, T. & Tovey, H. (eds.), *Poverty in Rural Ireland; A Political Economy Perspective,* Dublin: Combat Poverty Agency.

CWC – see Community Workers' Co-operative.

Dalal-Clayton, B. & Bass, S. (2002). *Sustainable Development Strategies: A Resource Book,* Paris: Earthscan OECD.

Department for Communities & Local Government (UK) (2007). *e-Transformation Programme: e-Planning Blueprint,* London: Her Majesty's Stationery Office, available at http://www.communities.gov.uk/documents/planningandbuilding/doc /158601.doc, accessed 2.11.2007.

Department of Agriculture & Food (1999). *Ensuring the Future: A Strategy for Rural Development in Ireland,* White Paper on Rural Development, Dublin: Government Publications.

Department of Arts, Heritage, Gaeltacht & the Islands (2003). *National Biodiversity Plan,* Dublin: Government Publications.

Department of Community, Rural & Gaeltacht Affairs (2000). *White Paper on Supporting Voluntary Activity,* Dublin: Government Publications.

Department of Environment & Local Government (1998). *Report of the Task Force on the Integration of Local Government & Local Development Systems,* Dublin: Government Publications.

Department of Environment & Local Government (1999). *Preparing the Ground: Guidelines for the Progress from Strategy Groups to the County/City Development Boards,* Dublin: Government Publications.

Department of Environment & Local Government (2000). *A Shared Vision for County/City Development Boards: Guidelines for the CDB Strategies for Economic, Social & Cultural Development,* Dublin: Government Publications.

Department of Environment & Local Government (2001). *Towards Sustainable Local Communities: Guidelines on Local Agenda 21,* Dublin: Government Publications.

Department of Finance (1999). *National Development Plan 2000- 2006,* Dublin: Government Publications, also available at http://www.ndp.ie.

Department of Social & Family Affairs (2003). *National Action Plan against Poverty & Social Exclusion 2003–2005,* Dublin: Government Publications.

Department of the Environment (1996). *Better Local Government: A Programme for Change,* Dublin: Government Pubications.

Department of the Environment, Heritage & Local Government (2007). *Development Plans – Guidelines for Planning Authorities,* Dublin: Government Publications,

available at http://www.environ.ie/en/Publications/DevelopmentandHousing/
Planning/, accessed 2.11.2007.

DoAHGI – see Department of Arts, Heritage, Gaeltacht & the Islands.

DoCRGA – see Department of Community, Rural & Gaeltacht Affairs.

DoE – see Department of the Environment.

DoEHLG – see Department of the Environment, Heritage & Local Government.

DoELG – see Department of Environment & Local Government.

DoE-UK – see Department of the Environment (UK).

Erickson, E. (undated). *Erickson's Psychosocial Stages Summary Chart*, available from
http:///psychology.about.com/library/bl_psychosocial_summary.htm, accessed
15.1.2008.

European Parliament & Council of the European Union (2001). *Directive 2001/42/EC:
The Assessment of the Effects of Certain Plans & Programmes on the Environment*,
available from http://www.environ.ie/DOEI/DOEIPol.nsf/0/
b8aeb091f741ee9c80256f5d004cd61c/$FILE/0142_en.pdf, accessed 24.3.2006.

Fainstein, S.S. (2000). 'New directions in planning theory', *Urban Affairs Review*,
Vol.35, Issue 4, March, pp.451-78.

Fisher, R. & Ury, W. (1983). *Getting to Yes: Negotiating Agreement Without Giving In*,
New York: Penguin Books.

Forde, C. (2005). 'Participatory democracy or pseudo-participation? Local
government reform in Ireland', *Local Government Studies*, Vol.31, No.2.

Forester, J. (1989). *Planning in the Face of Power*, Berkeley: University of California
Press.

Frazer, H. (1996). 'The role of community development in local development' in
Curtin, C. (ed.), *Partnership in Action: The Role of Community Development &
Partnership in Ireland*, Galway: Community Workers Co-operative.

Fung, A. & Wright, E.O. (eds.) (2003). *Deepening Democracy: Institutional Innovations in
Empowered Particpatory Governance*, London: Verso.

Galway County Council (2002). *Draft County Development Plan*, Galway: Galway
County Council.

Galway County Council (2004). *Kinvara Local Area Plan*, Galway: Galway County
Council.

Gaventa, J. (2002). 'Exploring citizenship, participation and accountability', *Institute of
Development Studies Bulletin*, Vol.33.

Glaser, B. & Strauss, A.L. (1967). *The Discovery of Grounded Theory: Strategies for
Qualitative Research*, Chigago: Aldine.

Goetz, A.M & Gaventa, J. (2001). *Bringing Citizen Voice & Client Focus into Service
Delivery*, IDS Working paper 138, Brighton: Institute of Development Studies,
University of Sussex.

Government of Ireland (2002). *National Spatial Strategy*, Dublin: Government
Publications.

Government of Ireland (2004). *Bunreacht na hÉireann / Constitution of Ireland*, Dublin:
Government Publications.

Griffin, E.M. (1997). *A First Look at Communication Theory*, 3rd edition, New York: McGraw-Hill.

Harris, N. (2002). 'Collaborative planning: From theoretical foundations to practice forms' in Allmendinger, P. & Tewdwr-Jones, M. (eds.), *Planning Futures: New Directions for Planning Theory*, Oxford: Routledge.

Healey, P. (1997). *Collaborative Planning: Shaping Places in Fragmented Societies*, Vancouver: VBC Press.

Hirst, P. (2000). 'Governance and democracy' in Pierre, J. (ed.), *Debating Governance. Authority, Steering & Democracy*, Oxford: Oxford University Press, pp. 13-35.

Humphreys, E. (2005). 'Social capital: Mediating conditions to create "successful" neighbourhoods' in *Civic & Social Life in the Suburbs Conference*, National University of Ireland, Maynooth, available at http://sociology.nuim.ie/documents/Humphreyspaper.pdf, accessed 15.1.2008.

IIED – see International Institute for Environment & Development.

Illsley, B. (2002). *Planning with Communities: A Good Practice Guide*, London: Royal Town Planning Institute.

Innes, J.E. & Booher, D.E. (2000). *Collaborative Dialogue as a Policy-making Strategy*, Working Paper 2000-05, Berkeley: Institute of Urban & Regional Development, University of California at Berkeley.

IPA – see Institute of Public Administration.

Jackson, J.A. & Haase. T. (1996). 'Demography & the distribution of deprivation in rural Ireland' in Curtin, C., Haase, T. & Tovey, H. (eds.), *Poverty in Rural Ireland: A Political Economy Perspective*, Dublin: Combat Poverty Agency.

Kende-Robb, C. (2005). *Participation & the World Bank: Mobilizing Parliamentarians for Democracy*, presentation, 12 June, Washington D.C.: World Bank.

Khanya (1999). *Rural Planning for Sustainable Livelihoods in South Africa*, available at www.khanya-aicdd.org, accessed 20.1.2008.

Komito, L. (1983). 'Development plan rezonings: The political pressures', in Blackwell, J. & Convery, F. (eds.), *Promise & Performance: Irish Environmental Policies Analysed*, Dublin: Resource & Environmental Policy Centre, University College Dublin, available at http://www.ucd.ie/lis/staff/komito/rezoning.htm, accessed 2.11.2007.

Lewin, K. (1946). 'Action research and minority problems', *Journal of Social Issues*, Vol.2, pp.34-46.

Losh, S.C. (2005). *The Role of Personality & Social Factors*, available at http://edp5285-01.sp05.fsu.edu/Guide5.html, accessed 15.1.2008.

Lynch, C. (2003). 'Capacity and community: The balance between the social and the environmental in a specific cultural context', in Persson, L.A., Ahlander, A.S. & Westlund, H. (eds.), *Local Responses to Global Changes: Economic & Social Development in Northern Europe's Countryside*, Stockholm: National Institute for Working Life.

MacCarthaigh, M. (2003). *Two Sides of the One Coin? Representative & Participatory Democracy in Irish Local Authorities*, IPA Food for Thought / Local Authority Unit paper, Dublin: Institute of Public Administration.

Manaster, G. J. & Corsini, R.J. (1995). *Individual Psychology: Theory & Practice*, 2nd edition, Chicago: Adler School of Professional Psychology.

McGee, R. *et al.* (2003). *Legal Framework for Citizen Participation*, Brighton: Institute of Development Studies, University of Sussex.

Moseley, M., Cherret, T. & Cawley, M., (2001). 'Local partnerships for rural development: Ireland's experience in context', *Irish Geography*, Vol.34, No.2.

Muddiman, D. (2000). 'Theories of social exclusion and the public library' in Muddiman, D. (ed.), *Open to All?: The Public Library & Social Exclusion*, Vol.3, London: The Council for Museums, Archives & Libraries.

*National Development Plan* – see Department of Finance (1999).

National Economic & Social Council (1994). *New Approaches to Rural Development*, Dublin: Government Publications.

National Economic & Social Forum (1997). *Rural Renewal: Combating Social Exclusion*, Report No. 12, Dublin: Government Publications.

National Economic & Social Forum (2003). *The Policy Implications of Social Capital*, Report No.28, Dublin: Government Publications.

NESC – see National Economic & Social Council.

NESF – see National Economic & Social Forum.

O'Connell, M. (ed.) (1993). *The Civil Deficit in Ireland: People Power*, Proceedings of the third annual Daniel O'Connell Workshop, Dublin: Institute of Public Administration.

O'Neill, S. (1998). 'Local partnerships, sustainable development and Agenda 21', in Community Workers Co-operative, *Local Development in Ireland: Policy Implications for the Future*, Galway: Community Workers Co-operative.

O'Carroll, J.P. (2002). 'Culture lag and democratic deficit in Ireland: Or, "Dat's outside de terms of d'agreement"', *Community Development Journal*, Vol.37, pp.10-19.

ODPM – see Office of the Deputy Prime Minister.

OECD – see Organisation for Economic Co-operation & Development.

Office of the Deputy Prime Minister (UK) (2003). *Participatory Planning for Sustainable Communities: International Experience in Mediation, Negotiation & Engagement in Making Plans*, available at http://www.communities.gov.uk/publications/planningandbuilding/participatory-planning, accessed 17.1.2008.

Office of the Deputy Prime Minister (UK) (2004). *Community Involvement in Planning: The Government's Objectives*, London: Her Majesty's Stationery Office, available at http://www.communities.gov.uk/publications/planningandbuilding/communityinvolvement, accessed 17.1.2008.

Organisation for Economic Co-operation & Development (2001). *Citizens as Partners: Information, Consultation & Public Participation in Policy-Making*, Paris: Organisation for Economic Co-operation & Development.

Pennington, M. (2002). 'A Hayekian liberal critique of collaborative planning' in Allmendinger, P. & Tewdwr-Jones, M. (eds.), *Planning Futures: New Directions in Planning Theory*, Oxford: Routledge, pp. 187-205.

Piachaud, D. (2002). *Capital & the Determinants of Poverty & Social Exclusion*, CASE Paper 60, London: Centre for Analysis of Social Exclusion.

Pobal (1999). *Local Development Social Inclusion Programme Guidelines 2000- 2006*, Dublin: Pobal, available at http://www.pobal.ie/media/ LDSIPGUIDELINESFINAL.pdf, accessed 1.4.2008.

Pobal (2003). *Community Work in a Rural Setting: An Examination of Community Work under the Local Development Social Inclusion Programme*, Dublin: Pobal.

Pringle, D. (2002). 'The geographical distribution of poverty in Ireland', in *Signposts to Rural Change*, Proceedings of Rural Development Conference, Dublin: Teagasc, pp.152-164.

Putnam, R. (1994). *Making Democracy Work*, Princeton, NJ: Princeton University Press.

Scott-Ladd, B. & Marshall, V. (2004). 'Participation in decision-making: A matter of context?', in *Leadership & Organization Development Journal*, Vol.25, No.8, pp.646-662.

Senge, P.M. (1990). *The Fifth Discipline: The Art & Practice of the Learning Organisation*, New York: Doubleday.

Silvera, I. (2000). 'Guide to taking part in planning appeals', *Planning Inspectorate Journal*, available at http://www.planning-inspectorate.gov.uk/pins/ publications/journals /archive/21_journal/pins21_engaging.htm, accessed 14.1.2006.

Skeffington, A.M. (1969). *People & Planning: Report of the Committee on Public Participation in Planning*, London, Her Majesty's Stationery Office.

Strauss, A.L. & Corbin, J. (1998). *Basics of Qualitative Research: Grounded Theory Procedures & Techniques*, Newbury Park, CA: Sage.

Taskforce on Active Citizenship (2007). *Report of the Taskforce on Active Citizenship*, Dublin: Government Publications.

Taylor, M. (2003). *Public Policy in the Community*, New York: Palgrave Macmillan.

Thompson, J. (1995). *Participatory Approaches in Government Bureaucracies: Facilitating the Process of Institutional Change*, London: International Institute for Environment & Development, London

Tovey, H., Haase, T. & Curtin, C. (1996). 'Understanding rural poverty' in Curtin, C., Haase, T., & Tovey, H. (eds.) *Poverty in Rural Ireland; A Political Economy Perspective*, Dublin: Oak Tree Press / Combat Poverty Agency.

UNECE – see United Nations Economic Commission for Europe.

United Nations (1992). *Local Agenda 21 Agreement: Report of the United Nations Conference on Environment & Development*, available from http://www.un.org/ documents/ga/conf151/aconf15126-1annex1.htm, acessed 10.6.2006.

United Nations Economic Commission for Europe (1998). *Access to Information, Public Participation in Decision-making & Access to Justice in Environmental Matters* (Aarhus Convention), available from http://www.unece.org/env/pp/, accessed 5.6.2006.

Varley, T. & Curtin, C. (2004). *Power, Populism & Partnership in Rural Ireland*, paper to conference 'Social Partnership: A New Kind of Governance?' at NUI Maynooth.

Varley, T. (2006). 'Negotiating power and powerlessness: Community interests and partnership in rural Ireland' in Healy, S., Reynolds, B. & Collins, M. (eds.), *Social Policy in Ireland: Principles, Practice, Problems*, Dublin: The Liffey Press.

Waterford County Council (2002). *County Development Strategy for 2002-2012*, Waterford: Waterford County Council.

Webster, C. & Ougham, H. (1998). 'Strengthening decision-making for sustainable development', report of a workshop held at Eynsham Hall, Oxford, available at http://www.sussex.ac.uk/Units/gec/pubs/reps/ decision.htm#2, accessed 28.12.2005.

*White Paper on Rural Development* – see Department of Agriculture & Food (1999).

Wolcott, H.F. (1994). *Transforming Qualitative Data: Description, Analysis & Interpretation*, Thousand Oaks, CA: Sage.

# FURTHER READING

Abram, S. & Cowell, R. (undated). *Community Planning in the United Kingdom: An Introduction,* available at http://www.shef.ac.uk/communityplanning/ UKcommunityplanning.

Beresford, P. & Croft, S. (1993). *Citizen Involvement: A Practical Guide for Change,* London: Palgrave Macmillan.

Callanan, M. (2003). 'Where stands local government?', in Callanan, M. & Keogan, J. (eds.), *Local Government in Ireland: Inside Out,* Dublin: Institute of Public Administration.

Callanan, M., O'Keeffe, A. & Byrne, P. (2004). *Review of the Operation of Strategic Policy Committees,* Dublin: Department of the Environment & Local Government.

Chambers, R. (1983). *Rural Development: Putting the Last First,* London: Intermediate Technology Publications.

Colin Buchanan & Partners Ltd & Mike Shanahan & Associates (2003). *Cork Rural Design Guide: Building a New House in the Countryside,* Cork: Cork County Council.

Collins, N. & Mack, N. (1996). 'Public participation and risk-taking: A case study of farm households', *International Journal of Social Economics,* Vol.23, No.12, pp.15-29.

Crickley, S. (1998). 'Local development and local governance: Challenges for the future', in Name?, ?. (ed.), *Local Development in Ireland: Policy Implications for the Future,* Galway: Community Workers Co-operative.

Curtin, C., Haase, T. & Tovey, H. (1996). *Poverty in Rural Ireland: A Political Economy Perspective,* Dublin: Oak Tree Press / Combat Poverty Agency.

Department of Food, Business & Development, University College Cork (2003). *Evaluation of the Kinvara Integrated Area Planning Project,* unpublished, Cork: University College Cork.

Galway County Council (2003). *Kinvara & Eyrecourt Lead the Way: Community Planning Experience,* leaflet prepared by Tipperary Institute & Galway Co Council.

Healy, S.J. & Reynolds, B. (1992). *Power, Participation & Exclusion,* Dublin: Justice Commission.

Humphreys, E. (2006). *Social Capital & Quality of Life in Disadvantaged Urban Neighbourhoods: A Critical Analysis,* presentation to Combat Poverty Agency seminar.

Knippen, J.T. & Green, T.B. (1995). 'How to use participative planning', *Management Development Review,* Vol.8, No.4, pp.32-35.

Martin, J. (undated). *Strategic Environmental Assessment: Integration into plan-making*, Dublin: Department of Environment, Heritage & Local Government, available at http://www.irishplanninginstitute.ie/downloads/J%20Martin.doc, accessed 24.3.2006.

Montgomery, J. (2005). 'Creativity, wealth creation, and place (city dynamics), *Town & Country Planning*, Vol.74, No.1.

National Economic & Social Council (1997). *Population Distribution & Economic Development: Trends & Policy Implications*, Dublin: National Economic & Social Council.

Parnell, J. & Crandall, W. (2001). 'Rethinking participative decision-making', *Personnel Review*, Vol.30, No.5, pp.523-535.

Randell, M. (2004). 'Constructing participation spaces', *Community Development Journal*, Vol.39, No.2, pp. 144-155.

Richardson, A. (1983). *Participation: Concepts on Social Policy One*, London: Routledge.

Ryan, M. (1999). 'The role of social process in participative decision-making in an international context, *Participation & Empowerment: An International Journal*, Vol.7, No.2, pp.33-42.

Walsh, J., Craig, S. & McCafferty, D. (1998). *Local Partnerships for Social Inclusion?* Dublin: Oak Tree Press / Combat Poverty Agency.

# INDEX